BUILDING
TEAMWORK
IN YOUR
MARRIAGE

FAMILYLIFE
HOMEBUILDERS
COUPLES SERIES

BUILDING TEAMWORK IN YOUR MARRIAGE

ROBERT LEWIS

GROUP LEADER'S GUIDE

"UNLESS THE LORD BUILDS THE HOUSE
THEY LABOR IN VAIN WHO BUILD IT."
Psalm 127:1

Gospel Light

How to
Let the Lord
Build Your House
and not labor in vain

FamilyLife is a part of Campus Crusade for Christ International, an evangelical Christian organization founded in 1951 by Bill Bright. FamilyLife was started in 1976 to help fulfill the Great Commission by strengthening marriages and families and then equipping them to go to the world with the gospel of Jesus Christ. Our FamilyLife Marriage Conference is held in most cities throughout the United States and is one of the fastest-growing marriage conferences in America today. Information on all resources offered by FamilyLife may be obtained by either writing or calling us at the address and telephone number listed below.

■

The HomeBuilders Couples Series: A small-group Bible study dedicated to making your family all that God intended.

Building Teamwork in Your Marriage—Leader's Guide
ISBN 0-8307-1615-7

Dennis Rainey, Director
FamilyLife
P.O. Box 23840
Little Rock, AR 72221-3840
(501) 223-8663

FAMILYLIFE

A Ministry of Campus Crusade for Christ International
Bill Bright, Founder and President

Published by Gospel Light, Ventura, California 93006

CONTENTS

FOCUS: Men and women are more than noticeably different. Understanding and responding to these deeper differences is important to building a good marriage.

FOCUS: Women are, by creation, different from men. These differences generate special needs—needs which a husband is uniquely called upon to fulfill.

Focus: Men are, by creation, different from women. These differences generate special needs—needs which a wife is uniquely called upon to fulfill.

ACKNOWLEDGMENTS

A hearty thank-you and a special word of recognition needs to be recorded here to those supportive individuals who helped make this Bible study a reality.

My wife, Sherard, of course, tops any list. No one has given my life more encouragement and energy than she has. No one provides more support to endeavors like this one than she does. Sherard is chiefly responsible for so much of the "right" in my life. A helper indeed!

Dennis Rainey is the visionary behind The HomeBuilders Couples Series. Thank you, Dennis, for your vote of confidence in allowing me this opportunity. You are a great friend, and I count it a real privilege to be serving next to you.

As my personal assistant, Ann Blair has been indispensable. It's not just that she typed and retyped many revisions of the original manuscript—it's the attitude with which she did so. Ann also offered many helpful suggestions.

I owe Julie Denker of FamilyLife many thank-yous, too. Julie helped push this project to completion. She also spent great amounts of time shaping this study into its final form with her excellent revisionist hands.

I also want to single out Ray Williams. Ray is a special friend who has consistently been available as a sounding board for new ideas and honest evaluation. Ray, I appreciate your insight and your patience.

To the many groups around the country who first piloted this project—thanks for your feedback. You *did* make significant contributions. I especially want to thank Ed and Judy Ligon for their encouragement.

Finally, I want to thank a gracious group of people known as Fellowship Bible Church in Little Rock, Arkansas. It has been a unique and special privilege to serve you these past 10 years. To you I dedicate this study.

FOREWORD

Webster defines the word "crisis" as a turning point, a critical turn in a disease. As we move into the 1990s, we are experiencing a crisis in the roles of husbands and wives.

The turning point has occurred because of a massive movement to redefine what it means to be a man or a woman, a husband or a wife. If we who are in the Christian community are to survive the onslaught of this movement, then we must return to our biblical moorings for stability and strength. That is why this study in The HomeBuilders Couples Series is so important—it gives couples a biblical definition and description of the husband's and wife's responsibility.

Robert Lewis is on target in one of the hottest issues facing Christian marriages. He is a profound biblical thinker, and his insights on the "battle of the sexes" will help you understand your mate in new ways. Because of his vast experience—over nearly 20 years—with couples, his practical solutions are workable and achievable. Robert's material will truly liberate many marriages to become all that God intended.

Dennis Rainey
Director of FamilyLife

INTRODUCTION

ABOUT THE HOMEBUILDERS COUPLES SERIES

What is the purpose of The HomeBuilders Series?

Do you remember the first time you fell in love? That junior high—or elementary school—"crush" stirred your affections with little or no effort on your part. We use the term "falling in love" to describe the phenomenon of suddenly discovering our emotions have been captured by someone delightful.

Unfortunately, our society tends to make us think that all loving relationships should be equally as effortless. Thus, millions of couples, Christians included, approach their marriage certain that the emotions they feel will carry them through any difficulties. And millions of couples quickly learn that a good marriage does not automatically happen.

Otherwise intelligent people, who would not think of buying a car, investing money, or even going to the grocery store without some initial planning, enter into marriage with no plan of how to make their marriage succeed.

But God has already provided the plan, a set of blueprints for a truly godly marriage. His plan is designed to enable two people to grow together in a mutually satisfying relationship, and then to look beyond their own marriage to others. Ignoring this plan leads to isolation and separation between husband and wife—the pattern so evident in the majority of homes today. Even when great energy is expended, failure to follow God's blueprints results in wasted effort, bitter disappointment—and, in far too many cases, divorce.

In response to this need in marriages today, FamilyLife of Campus Crusade for Christ has created a series of small-group Bible studies for couples called The HomeBuilders Couples Series. The series is designed for small-group studies and is easily adaptable to larger groups such as adult Sunday School classes. It is planned to answer one question for couples:

How do you build a distinctively Christian marriage?

It is our hope that in answering this question with the biblical blueprints for building a home, we will see the development of growing, thriving marriages filled with the love of Jesus Christ.

FamilyLife of Campus Crusade for Christ is committed to strengthening your family. We hope The HomeBuilders Couples Series will assist you and your church as it equips couples in building godly homes.

What is this study intended to accomplish?

Couples who participate in these sessions will find that the experience:

- Stimulates them to examine what Scripture says about how to construct a solid, satisfying marriage.
- Allows them to interact with each other on a regular basis about significant issues in their marriages.
- Encourages them to interact with other couples, establishing mutual accountability for growth efforts.
- Motivates them to take specific actions which have been valuable to couples desiring to build stronger homes.
- Creates accountability to others for growth in their marriages.

Why is accountability so important?

Accountability is a scriptural principle that tells us to "be subject to one another in the fear of Christ" (Ephesians 5:21). This means I choose to submit my life to the scrutiny of another person in order to gain spiritual strength, growth and balance.

Accountability means asking another person for advice. It means giving him the freedom to make honest observations and evaluations about you. It means you're teachable and approachable. True accountability involves letting another person into the interior of your life.

When a person joins a small group, he is opening himself up for at least a small measure of accountability. Our experience has shown that many group members will make commitments to apply aspects of the studies to their lives, but will never follow through on those commitments. As a small-group leader, establishing an environment of friendly accountability can help your group members get the most out of this study.

Look for some hints on establishing accountability in the "Tips for Leading Your Group" section.

What impact has The HomeBuilders Couples Series had in marriages?

Since we published the first HomeBuilders study in 1987, we've continually heard stories about couples whose marriages were revitalized and, in some cases, even saved. Here are some examples:

> "We started our HomeBuilders group as a follow-up to the Video FamilyLife Conference presented at our church. We have developed a good openness among the group members. It has brought problem areas to the surface and given us a greater sense of awareness of our responsibility toward our mate. One couple travels as far as an hour to attend!"
>
> Pastor, Washington

> "We're using *Building Your Marriage* and *Mastering Your Money in Marriage* in our Sunday school classes, both for newlyweds and as a marriage renewal class. I have seen couples open communication lines for the first time in a long time as a result of their involvement."
>
> Bill Willits
> Minister to Married Adults
> First Baptist Church
> Atlanta, Ga.

> "We've led three studies now, and in each one of those we have seen ourselves grow. You really do co-learn."
>
> Doug Grimm
> Playa Del Rey, Calif.

> "I've built my family ministry around the FamilyLife Conference and the HomeBuilders. It makes biblically-mind-

ed, servant-minded people who are useful for advancing the kingdom and leadership of the kingdom."

Jeff Rhodes, pastor
First Presbyterian Church
Winterhaven, Fla.

"Nine weeks of the HomeBuilders class turned everything around in our relationship. It was a real miracle. The walls came down and the masks came off. We were able to discuss matters we had swept under the carpet years ago that our enemy was consistently using to destroy the love God had designed for us since the beginning of time....

"The HomeBuilders class really works. Here is why: HomeBuilders not only shows you why, and tells you how, it teaches a way to alter your life-style so these great truths become a part of everyday living.

"We have truly overcome isolation and are building toward oneness in our marriage. We have learned how to yield to God and the leading of His Holy Spirit instead of our own selfish desires...the romance is back and the intimacy is growing every day. HomeBuilders has really given us the 'wisdom' we were looking for in our marriage.

"It is absolutely the best thing that has ever happened to us since becoming Christians 18 years ago. It changed our lives at a time I was just ready to accept apathy for parts of my marriage, figuring there was no way to ever change."

Alan and Lanette Hauge
Playa Del Rey, Calif.

How does this study fit into a strategy for building Christian marriages?

While this study has great value in itself, it is only the first step in a long-term process of growth. If people complete these sessions and then gradually return to their previous patterns of living, little or no good will result. Continued effort is required for people to initiate and maintain new directions in their marriages.

It is our belief, also, that no couple can truly build a Christian home and marriage without a strong commitment and involvement in a local church. The church provides the daily spiritual direction and equipping necessary for a truly godly marriage.

FamilyLife is committed to changing the destiny of the family and providing quality resources to churches and individuals to build distinctively Christian marriages. In addition to The Home-Builders Couples Series, we offer:

- "FamilyLife Today," our daily radio show with Dennis Rainey. This half-hour broadcast offers biblical, practical tips for building your family with a foundation in Christ.
- The FamilyLife Marriage Conference, a weekend getaway for couples to learn how to experience oneness in their marriages.
- The FamilyLife Parenting Conference, in which parents learn practical ways to raise their children to know and love the Lord.
- The Urban Family Conference, a shorter version of the FamilyLife Marriage Conference that is geared to the needs of African-American families.
- Numerous materials to help you grow as a family and reach out to others.

Can this study be used in other settings besides small groups?

Yes! With capable leadership, this study may be used effectively in other settings. For example:

- A counselor could use it with a couple.
- Two couples who know each other well could work through it together.
- You could go through the study with your mate. (We encourage you, however, to make your ultimate goal that of taking others through this study, or participating in a small group. Accountability is essential for godly marriages.)
- A Sunday School leader can adapt it to a larger group setting. For some suggestions on how this can be done, refer to the section titled, "Using This Study in a Sunday School Setting."

Does each session follow a format?

Yes. The following outline gives a quick look at how the sessions are structured:

FOCUS: a statement of the overall focus of the session you will be studying.

WARM UP: a time to help people get to know each other, review the past session and begin the new study.

BLUEPRINTS: the biblical content of the session.

CONSTRUCTION: the application of the session—a small project done privately as a couple during the session.

HOMEBUILDERS PRINCIPLES: summary points made throughout the study.

MAKE A DATE: a time for couples to decide when they will complete their **HomeBuilders Project**.

HOMEBUILDERS PROJECT: a 60-90 minute project to be completed at home before the next session.

RECOMMENDED READING: suggestions for use of several books to get maximum value from the study.

Although this format may vary slightly from session to session, you should familiarize yourself with it so that you are aware of the purpose of each segment of the study. Explaining the segments to your group will also aid them in understanding the session's content.

How is the Bible used in this study?

As you proceed through this study, you will notice that the Bible is regarded as the final authority on the issues of life and marriage. Although written centuries ago, this Book still speaks clearly and powerfully about the conflicts and struggles men and women face. The Bible is God's Word and contains His blueprints for building a godly home and for dealing with the practical issues of living.

While Scripture has only one primary interpretation, there may be several appropriate applications. Some of the passages used in this series were not originally written with marriage in mind, but they can be applied practically to the husband-wife relationship.

Encourage each group member to have a Bible with him for each session. The *New American Standard Bible*, the *New International Version*® and the *New King James Version* are three excellent English versions which make the Bible easy to understand.

What are the ground rules for these sessions?

These sessions are designed to be enjoyable and informative—and nonthreatening. Three simple ground rules will help ensure that everyone feels comfortable and gets the most out of the study:

1. Share nothing about your marriage which will embarrass your mate.
2. You may "pass" on any question you do not want to answer.
3. Complete the **HomeBuilders Projects** (questions for each couple to discuss and act on) between each session. Share one result at the next group meeting.

What is the purpose of this leader's guide?

This book and the suggestions we make are designed to cause your creative juices to flow, not cramp your style. You will undoubtedly come up with some creative ways to instruct and teach this material. That's fine. Don't let these recommendations force you into a box.

If, however, you find it difficult to be creative as a facilitator, this guide will relieve your fears. In it you will find ideas, questions and tips that will help you keep the study moving.

The entire text of the study guide (including **Construction** and **HomeBuilders Projects**) is reprinted here, along with the tips for the leader and answers to the study guide questions. All answers, tips and notes appear in italics to distinguish them from the study guide material. As a couple, use this guide to prepare for the session, regardless of the type of leader you are. One good question on a hot topic can spawn great discussion and interaction. Remember, this study is for these couples' marriages and their application.

① Goals Goals
② Fellowship
③ Not mean bad - means better

TIPS FOR LEADING YOUR GROUP

What does it take to lead this study?

First, you and your mate need to commit to each other and to God that this study will be a major priority for both of you.

Second, you will need to work together to enlist other couples to participate in the group.

Third, one of you will need to give time (at least one or two hours) each week to prepare for the session while the other takes the initiative to stay in touch with group members and to handle all the details of hospitality.

And **fourth**, we recommended that you pray regularly for each couple in your group.

What is the leader's job?

Your role is that of "facilitator"—a directive guide who encourages people to think, to discover what Scripture says and to interact with others in the group. You are not a teacher or lecturer—your job is to help the group members glean biblical truth and apply it to their lives.

At the same time, however, you don't want to let group members ramble aimlessly or pool their ignorance. You'll need to familiarize yourself with the material so that you know where the discussion is headed and so that you can provide answers when needed. The directions in this leader's guide will help you keep each session moving.

What is the best setting for this group to meet?

Your living room is probably the best place to use for a small group. Inviting couples to your home is usually easier and friendlier than trying to get them to come to a room at church. You need a room where everyone can sit comfortably and see and hear each other.

Avoid letting couples or individuals sit outside the group; they will not feel included. The seating arrangement is very important to discussion and involvement. If your home will not work, see if another couple in the group is willing to host the sessions.

What about refreshments?

If you want a comfortable, relaxed setting that encourages people to get to know one another, something to sip and swallow is almost essential. But food should not become the focus of the session. Depending on the time of your meeting, you may find it works well to serve a beverage and light "munchies" as people arrive, then offer a dessert at the close of the study to encourage people to continue talking with each other for a while.

What time schedule should we plan to follow?

A two-hour block is best. The time for the actual study is 60-90 minutes. The longer time period allows you to move at a more relaxed pace through each part of the session.

Once the people in your group get to know each other and interaction gets underway, you may find it difficult to complete a session in the time allotted. It is not necessary that every question be covered and many are intended to stimulate thought, not to result in exhaustive discussion and resolution of the issue. Be sensitive to your use of time and be careful not to make comments about time pressure which will make the group feel rushed. For example:

- When you need to move the discussion to the next item, say something like, "We could probably talk about that question the rest of the evening, but we need to consider several other important questions that bear on this issue."

- When it's necessary to reduce or eliminate the time spent on a later question, simply say, "You can see that there are several more questions we could have moved on to discuss, but I felt we were making real progress, so I chose to spend some extra time on the earlier points."

You will find, as you prepare and review for each session, that some questions or sections are more relevant to your group than other portions of the study. Pace your study in such a way that those questions which must be addressed are not rushed.

You are the leader of your group and know the needs of the individual couples best. But keep in mind that the Holy Spirit will have an agenda for couples which you will never know about.

"The mind of man plans his way, but the Lord directs his steps" (Proverbs 16:9). Do your best to prepare and pray over the session and then leave the results to God.

Be sure to protect the application (**Construction**) time at the end of the session. Be aware of the common tendency to avoid taking action by getting embroiled in a discussion. Even if some issues are not fully resolved, encourage people to place the topic on hold and move on to planning specific actions to take. Personal application is at the heart of this study.

Plan up to an additional 30 minutes for fellowship, 5 or 10 minutes of which may precede the study and the remainder afterwards. When you invite people, tell them to plan on the total time. This avoids having people rush off and not get acquainted. During the school year 7:30-9:30 P.M. allows people to get home from work and get baby-sitters if needed.

Also, when you invite people to attend, let them know that the study will go for seven sessions. People like to know for how long they are committing themselves.

How many couples should be in a study group?
Four to seven couples, including you and your mate, is the optimum group size. Fewer than four may put too much pressure on some individuals, stifling their freedom to grow. More than seven will reduce the quality of relationships which can grow among all the couples involved, although there is still ample opportunity for couples to interact with each other and with other couples in the group.

Whom should we invite to participate?
The concepts in this study will benefit any couple, whether they are newlyweds, engaged, married many years or even just looking ahead to the possibilities of marriage. Leading the group will be easier if your group is made up of couples at similar stages in their relationships. The more they have in common, the easier it will be for them to identify with one another and open up in sharing.

On the other hand, it can also be helpful for a couple to gain a fresh viewpoint on marriage by interacting with a couple having significantly different experiences. In other words, if a couple is interested in building and maintaining a strong marriage, they belong in this study.

What if one partner doesn't want to participate?

Expect some people, especially some husbands, to attend the first session wishing they were someplace else. Some will be there just because their mate or another couple nagged them to come. Some may be suspicious of a "Bible" study. Others may be fearful of revealing any weaknesses in their marriage. And some may feel either that their marriage is beyond help or that they do not need any help.

You can dispel a great deal of anxiety and resistance at the first session. Simply begin by mentioning that you know there are probably some who came reluctantly. Share a few reasons people may feel that way, and affirm that regardless of why anyone has come, you are pleased each person is there.

Briefly comment on how the concepts in this study have helped you and your marriage and express your confidence that each person will enjoy the study and benefit from it. Also, assure the group that at no time will anyone be forced to share publicly. What each person shares is his or her choice—no one will be embarrassed.

Can a non-Christian participate in this study?

The study is definitely targeted at Christians, but many non-Christian couples have participated in it. You may find a non-Christian couple or individual who wants to build a strong marriage and is willing to participate. Welcome the non-Christian into your group and seek to get to know the person during the early weeks of the study.

Sometime during the study, schedule a time to meet with this person or couple privately to explain the principles on which this study is built. Share Christ and offer an opportunity to receive Him as Savior and Lord. We recommend "The Four Spiritual Laws" to help you explain how a person can know God. This information is included as an appendix to the study guide and the leader's guide.

Do you have any suggestions for guiding the discussion?

Keep the focus on what Scripture says, not on you or your ideas—or those of the group members, either. When someone disagrees with Scripture, affirm him or her for wrestling with the issue and point out that some biblical statements are hard to understand or to accept. Encourage the person to keep an open mind on the issue at least through the remainder of the study.

Avoid labeling an answer as "wrong"; doing so can kill the atmosphere for discussion. Encourage a person who gives a wrong or incomplete answer to look again at the question or the Scripture being explored. Offer a comment such as, "That's really close" or, "There's something else we need to see there." Or ask others in the group to respond.

How can I get all the people in my group to participate in the discussion?

■ A good way to encourage a nonparticipator to respond is to ask him or her to share an opinion or a personal experience rather than posing a question that can be answered "yes" or "no" or that requires a specific correct answer.

■ The overly talkative person can be kept in control by the use of devices that call for responses in a specific manner (and which also help group members get to know little things about each other):

"I'd like this question to be answered first by the husband of the couple with the next anniversary."

"...the wife of the couple who had the shortest engagement."

"...any husband who knows his mother-in-law's maiden name."

"...anyone who complained about doing the last session's project."

■ Other devices for guiding responses from the group include:

Go around the group in sequence with each person commenting about a particular question without repeating what anyone else has said.

Ask couples to talk with each other about a question, then have whichever partner has said the least so far in this session report on his or her answer.

Limit answers to one or two sentences—or to 30 seconds each.

How can I establish an environment of accountability?

From the outset, emphasize the importance of completing the **HomeBuilders Project** after each session. These projects give couples the opportunity to discuss what they've learned and apply it to their lives. The couples who complete these projects will get two or three times as much out of this study as will those who do not.

The most important thing you can do is state at the end of the first session that *at your next meeting you will ask each couple to share something they learned from the **HomeBuilders Project**. Then, at the next session, follow through on your promise.* If they know you are going to hold them accountable, they'll be more motivated to complete the projects. And they'll be glad they did!

Remember, though, to make this an environment of *friendly* accountability. You should emphasize how beneficial the projects are, and how much persons will grow in their marriage relationship if they complete them. State that you are not here to condemn, but to help. And when you begin the following session by asking each couple what they learned from the project, do it with an attitude of encouragement and forgiveness. Don't seek to embarrass anyone.

One way to establish friendly accountability and to help couples know each other better is to pair up the couples in your group and assign them to be prayer partners or accountability partners. Have them call each other at some point in between group meetings to exchange prayer requests and to see if they've completed their projects.

Another possibility to consider is making a special effort to hold the *men* accountable to be the initiator in completing the projects. You'd need to commit yourself to calling the men in between sessions.

What should I expect group members to do at the end of these sessions?

As you prepare this study, prayerfully consider each couple in your group and the most appropriate next step to recommend they take when the study is completed:

1. Encourage them to commit to participate in another Home-Builders study, such as *Building Your Mate's Self-Esteem.* (Dennis and Barbara Rainey have coauthored a best-selling book with this same title, *Building Your Mate's Self-Esteem.*) Decide whether you or someone else will lead the study and when you would schedule it. Since some people may not continue to the next study, it may be wise to schedule the other study after several more groups have completed this one. However, if you wait too long, you and your group members may lose the momentum built through this study.

2. Some couples in your group may be candidates to lead their own group in studying *Building Teamwork in Your Marriage.* Raise this possibility, even though their first reaction may be "We don't know enough to be leaders!" Assure them that sharing what they have learned with others is the best way to continue learning. And obviously, if you can lead this study, *they* certainly can as well. Remember, the more couples who go through this book, the more couples you will have ready for another one.

Expect many to continue on through The HomeBuilders Couples Series. Relationships established during this study will cause most group members to want to continue.

USING THIS STUDY IN A SUNDAY SCHOOL SETTING

Although this study is currently written for a small-group, home Bible study, with a few minutes of extra planning you can adapt it for a Sunday School class. Here are a few steps to take:

STEP ONE: Commit yourself to the small-group format. Many Sunday School classes are geared around a *teacher* format rather than a *small-group* format. In other words, class members learn biblical content from a speaker, and have little interaction with each other. The success of this HomeBuilders study, however, depends upon the small-group dynamic, with class members learning the content by discussing Scriptures themselves and by sharing personal experiences. As leader of the class, you'll need to be committed to making this small-group setting work.

STEP TWO: Explain to your class how this study is different from others. Tell them about the small-group format, and about the purpose of the series. Challenge them to commit themselves to coming each week. And explain the need to set aside an hour each week to complete the **HomeBuilders Projects**.

Another difference with a HomeBuilders study is the **Construction** project, in which couples meet individually for a few minutes during the study. While the classroom may not provide visual privacy as couples talk, the sound of numerous couples talking at once make it unlikely anyone will overhear someone's private conversation. In some cases the results of their work are to be shared. In a class situation, this sharing should be done in small groups, or ask for volunteers to share with the full class.

STEP THREE: Decide how you want to cover all the material in the time you have for Sunday School. The problem here is simple: These studies are written to last for 60-90 minutes. Most Sunday School classes are an hour long and that time normally includes announcements, singing and prayer. Here are three options to consider:

1. *Eliminate—for just these few weeks—the normal singing and announcements.* If you follow the shorter time guideline for each segment of the sessions, all the content and projects can fit in a 60-minute session.

   People who are used to slipping in late may need an extra nudge to get them there on time. The informal fellowship dimension which is vital to helping people feel at home in the group can be done to a degree before and after the session. The leader will need to be very sensitive to using that time wisely, since people will have other commitments that keep them from lingering.

2. *Look for ways to condense the actual study to about 45 minutes.* One way to accomplish this, of course, is to cut a few questions. Look through each lesson and determine what is most important to cover, and mark the questions that you think could be eliminated. Perhaps you can choose just one question from a **Warm Up** to use, for example.

   If you have more than one small group in your class, another option is to divide questions (or verses) among different groups for discussion, and then have them report briefly on their answers to the whole class.

3. *Divide each session in half and use two weeks of Sunday School for each one.* Go through each session ahead of time and determine a natural stopping place—at the end of one section of **Blueprints,** for example. Then pick up the session at that point next week.

   One thing to consider if you use this option is that you may need to come up with a new **Warm Up** question to use at the beginning of the second week for each session.

STEP FOUR: Determine how you're going to *divide* the class. If you have less than nine couples, you could have just one group. But if your class is larger, we suggest dividing it. You could either assign each couple to one group that it will meet with during the entire study, or you could divide the class into different groups each week.

STEP FIVE: Decide how you're going to *direct* the class. Do you want to appoint a leader for each group or do you prefer guiding the discussion from up front? If you do want to guide the discussion, you could switch back and forth between having the individuals answer questions to the whole class and answering them just within the small groups.

STEP SIX: Arrange your physical setting. Use a room where interaction in small groups and couples can easily occur. Leave adequate open space where people can mingle casually before and after the session. Set up chairs around tables or just in circles of six to eight. For variety in some sessions, you may want to set the chairs in a large semicircle (with more than one row if necessary). Avoid straight rows that leave people seeing only the backs of heads.

Plan to occasionally use a chalkboard, overhead projector or flip chart to emphasize key points, to focus attention on key questions or Scriptures and/or to place instructions for assignments to be done by individuals, couples or small groups. Be cautious about overuse of these tools, as they can set a "classroom" tone which may inhibit some people from full participation.

STEP SEVEN: Decide how you will set up an atmosphere of accountability. While the **HomeBuilders Projects** are done by couples at home, it is vital that a larger group size does not allow people to escape accountability for completing the assignments. One option is to pair each couple with another couple with whom they will agree to be accountable. Another plan is to divide the class into two or more teams. Each week require couples to turn in an affidavit that they completed their project. Tabulate the results. The team with the lowest completion rate must provide some agreed upon benefit (preferably edible) for the winning team at the end of the series.

ABOUT THIS
LEADER'S GUIDE

The entire text of the study guide is included in this book. At the beginning of each session, you'll find some general comments and suggestions. Then, beginning with the **Warm Up**, the text from the study guide is printed in normal type, while comments, answers to questions and tips are printed in italics.

Be sure to read all the leader's guide comments for each session before you lead it.

HOMEBUILDERS PRINCIPLES

HOMEBUILDERS PRINCIPLE #1:

The Scripture will make you wise in the way you live with your mate (Psalm 119:97-100).

HOMEBUILDERS PRINCIPLE #2:

True equality in a marriage is achieved when a husband and a wife come to understand, appreciate and honor each other's differentness.

HOMEBUILDERS PRINCIPLE #3:

The greatest need a woman has in her marriage is to be loved rightly.

HOMEBUILDERS PRINCIPLE #4:

Other than a man's relationship with the Lord, few things tell a man more about himself than does the respect of his wife.

HOMEBUILDERS PRINCIPLE #5:

It is crucial that a husband's leadership role be accurately defined before it can be accurately fulfilled.

HOMEBUILDERS PRINCIPLE #6:

Submission is a woman's spiritual *response* that encourages her husband to fulfill his spiritual role. Submission is essential to the man's success as a servant-leader.

HOMEBUILDERS PRINCIPLE #7:

It is crucial that a wife's role as helper and homemaker be accurately defined before it can be accurately fulfilled.

HOMEBUILDERS PRINCIPLE #8:

Honor and praise are the masculine counterparts to submission. They are essential to the wife's success as a helper-homemaker.

HOMEBUILDERS PRINCIPLE #9:

The Holy Spirit will be faithful to remind us of God's Word if we are faithful in learning it.

HOMEBUILDERS PRINCIPLE #10:

The fuel that most often energizes the flesh is our world (1 John 2:15; Jude 19).

HOMEBUILDERS PRINCIPLE #11:

The Holy Spirit helps fulfill in us what God requires of us in marriage.

HOMEBUILDERS PRINCIPLE #12:

The fuel that most energizes the Spirit is God's Word
(2 Timothy 3:16; Colossians 3:16a).

HOMEBUILDERS PRINCIPLE #13:

A husband and wife can resolve their gender differences, repond to unique needs and fulfill respective roles as they submit by faith to God's Spirit and live under His special influence (Ephesians 5:18).

HOMEBUILDERS PRINCIPLE #14:

You will leave in your children what you have lived out in your home.

HOMEBUILDERS PRINCIPLE #15:

A wise couple knows what life's most promising investments are.

THE HOMEBUILDERS
COUPLES SERIES

"Unless the Lord builds the house,
they labor in vain who build it."
Psalm 127:1

COMPREHENDING YOUR MATE'S DIFFERENTNESS

OBJECTIVES

You will help your group members increase their awareness and appreciation of male and female differences in marriage as you guide them to:

- Examine the biblical basis for awareness of male/female differences;
- Discuss common misconceptions which arise regarding male/female differences;
- Study biblical instructions for how husbands and wives are to respond to the male/female differences in a marriage; and
- Commit time and interest in studying this topic further in the weeks of this study.

OVERALL COMMENTS

1. This session sets the tone for the series. Become familiar with every item in the study guide as well as the following instructions. Use the time indicators for each section as a guide in pacing the session (the smaller number is for a 60-minute session, the larger number for a 90-minute session).
2. The main intent of Session One is to build the understanding that many of the differences that exist in marriages are the

result of male and female differentness. It was God who constructed men and women to be uniquely different from each other. Because these differences will not go away, the wise couple will acknowledge, understand and even honor them.

To bring couples to a proper comprehension of some of these important male/female differences, an accurate understanding of statements in Scripture is necessary. It is crucial that group members recognize Scripture as the essential source of our understanding of human nature and its expression in male and female distinctives. Throughout this study you will continually go to Scripture to define the differences, roles, needs and responses to one another.

3. Be prepared to jump in and soften the atmosphere if the group becomes heated in its discussion. This may not happen, but a discussion about male/female differences often brings out some sharp disagreements. On one hand, most people recognize some clear differences. On the other, they may have very different views on what causes those differences. Encourage everyone to express their opinion, but avoid letting it fall into an argument. You could say something like: "This discussion shows why this is such an important topic to consider. One problem is that for many years, researchers have insisted that male/female differences are totally the result of how individuals are raised. Now we're seeing more articles and research showing that many differences may actually be natural. What we want to do in this study is take a look at what the Bible says."

4. Try to make sure every couple has a copy of the *New American Standard Bible*. Many of the questions in these sessions focus on specific words and phrases within Scripture passages. If the group uses differing translations, the crucial focus of these words and phrases may be lost. Thus, it is extremely important to provide one common translation for everyone to use. Check with group members before the first session to see if they have the *New American Standard Bible*. You may need to secure copies from your local church or from friends for group members who do not have their own copy of this version.

5. Be sure you have a study guide for each individual.

STARTING THE FIRST SESSION

1. Start the session on time, even if everyone is not there yet.
2. Briefly share a few positive feelings about leading this study:

   - Express your interest in strengthening your own marriage.
   - Admit that your marriage is not perfect.
   - State that the concepts in this study have been helpful in your marriage.
   - Recognize that various individuals or couples may have been reluctant to come (pressured by spouse or friend, wary of a "Christian" group, sensitive about problems with marriage, stress in schedule that makes it difficult to set aside the time for this series, etc.).
   - Thank group members for their interest and willingness to participate.

3. Hand out the study guides if you haven't already done so, and give a quick overview of The HomeBuilders Couples Series and the study guide. Briskly leaf through the study guide and point out three or four topics and the benefits of studying them. Don't be afraid of doing a little selling here—people need to know how they personally are going to profit from the study. They also need to know where this series will take them, especially if they are even a little bit apprehensive about the group.
4. Explain the format for each session in no more than two or three minutes, using Session One as your example. Each session contains the following components:

Focus
A capsule statement of the main point of the session.

Warm Up
A time to get better acquainted with each other and
to begin thinking of the session topic.

Blueprints

Discovering God's purposes and plans for marriage.

HOMEBUILDERS PRINCIPLES

Summary points made throughout the study.

Construction

Applying something that was learned, usually
working as a couple.

Make a Date

A time to decide when during the week they will
complete the **HomeBuilders Project**.

HOMEBUILDERS PROJECT

An hour during the week when husband and wife
interact with the implications of what was learned.
These times are really the heart of the series.

Recommended Reading

Books that couples can read together to get
maximum benefit from the study.

5. Call attention to the "ground rules" for the sessions:
   a. Share nothing about your marriage which will embarrass
      your mate.
   b. You may "pass" on any question you do not want to
      answer.
   c. Complete the **HomeBuilders Project** (questions for each
      couple to discuss and act on) between each session.
      Share one result at the next group meeting.

NOTE: Beginning with the **Warm Up**, material that
appears in the study guide is presented in regular type
and added material for the leader appears in *italics*.

Focus

Men and women are more
than noticeably different.
Understanding and responding
to these deeper differences
is important to building
a good marriage.

Warm Up

(15-20 minutes)

*There are two **Warm Up** options provided for this session. The first activity is designed primarily for groups where the participants may not all know each other well. The alternative **Warm Up** is for groups whose members are already well acquainted and comfortable with each other.*

Welcome group members individually as they arrive. Introduce those who do not know each other and assist them in beginning some informal conversation. A choice of hot or cold beverage and a light refreshment will help people relax and begin to anticipate an enjoyable time together.

*Take ample time during the **Warm Up** for people to begin to feel comfortable with one another. Set the tone—and an example of the amount of time to talk—by sharing your responses first.*

If the group is too large to allow everyone to share, divide into two or more smaller groups to encourage full participation at the start of the session.

1. Introduce yourself to the group by sharing the following information:

a. name

b. occupation

c. years married

d. number of children (if any)

e. one expectation you have in joining this study

Use the space below to record your new knowledge of the others in the group.

An alternative to the previous **Warm Up** is the following exercise. You may choose to use this if your group is well acquainted with one another.

> *TIP: Introduce yourself to the group first, then guide the others in sharing their responses. Encourage people to record the information shared by others on the appropriate page in their study guides.*

2. Complete the following statement: My marriage has taught me some important things about the opposite sex. For instance ...

When you share what you have written, be sure to add *how* you came to this conclusion.

Blueprints

(25-35 minutes)

I. CREATIVE DIFFERENCES *(10-15 minutes)*

"And God created man in His own image, in the image of God He created him; male and female He created them" (Genesis 1:27).

It was a wonderful thing God did when He divided man into "male and female." He called His two creations "very good" (Genesis 1:31). The differences separating man as male and woman as female were intended to usher in many special blessings (Genesis 1:28). Unfortunately, with the fall of man, the blessings of the sexes became more a battle between the sexes. The unique qualities with which God endowed each gender now gave rise to misunderstanding and contention rather than completion and power.

To recapture what has been lost, we must first develop an understanding of, and then an appreciation for, God's design of mankind as "male and female." We are each married to someone who is both like us and yet unlike us. We each bear God's image but we express that image differently—as male and female. So to accurately comprehend and ultimately love the special differences these terms imply is of vital importance to any marriage. As we all know, these differences are not theoretical in nature but intensely practical. Therefore, becoming a student of the opposite sex is a great starting place for building a good marriage (or rebuilding a damaged one).

> ***TIP:*** *Call on a group member to read aloud Genesis 1:27 and the two paragraphs under Roman numeral I, "Creative Differences."*

II. PRACTICAL DIFFERENCES *(5 minutes)*

Below are a series of general observations social scientists have made regarding male and female differences.[1] Discuss with your group how each of these differences has at times manifested itself in your marriage. What misunderstandings (if any) have resulted because of them?

A. Women have a greater need of belonging; men have a greater need of achieving.

B. Women are more sensitive than men; the expressing of feelings is more important to them.

C. Men tend to see their work as extensions of themselves; women are apt to see their husband and family that way.

D. Men are more goal-oriented; women more need-oriented.

E. Men are more focused in their thinking; women are more intuitive in their thinking.

F. Women tend to require more frequent reassurance.

G. Men are more physical; women are more relational.

> *TIP: Be ready to share from your own experience if needed to stimulate group members to participate. Keep this interaction light, letting people feel comfortable in laughing at themselves and their reactions to differences with their mate. Continue similarly with the other observations.*

---

1. There will always be exceptions to any general observation. Exceptions, however, should not negate the truthfulness of these general observations nor undermine their helpfulness. For an excellent discussion on men's and women's differences, see Steven B. Clark's book, *Man and Woman in Christ: An Examination of the Roles of Men and Women in Light of Scripture and the Social Sciences* (Ann Arbor: Servant Books, 1980), pp. 371-448.

III. A CALL TO UNDERSTANDING
(10-15 minutes)

A. God never intended for male and female differences to divide husbands and wives or bring conflict between them. Quite the contrary; God's original intent was for us to appreciate and honor those unique qualities which our mates possess. The Scripture appeals to us to adopt this kind of perspective.

> "You husbands likewise, live with your wives in an understanding way, as with a weaker vessel,[2] since she is a woman; and grant her honor as a fellow heir of the grace of life, so that your prayers may not be hindered" (1 Peter 3:7).

What are the two major exhortations to husbands in this passage?

1.

2.

> ***ANSWER:*** *Understand your wife as a woman; grant her honor as a fellow-heir of Jesus Christ.*

B. The First Exhortation
1. How does the first exhortation in this passage call for a recognition of the differences between the sexes?

> ***ANSWER:*** *It is "since she is a woman" that a man needs understanding into her thoughts and feelings. This recognition goes all the way back to God's original creation when He created both female and male as unique from the other.*

---

2. "Weaker vessel" is most probably referring to a woman's physical strength as compared to that of a man's. Men generally have more muscle than women. Selfish men have used this superior physical strength as a means of subjugating and intimidating women.

2. If this first exhortation were being addressed to wives instead of husbands, would it be stated any differently? If so, how?

> ***ANSWER:*** *The basic thought would probably remain the same, although the phrase "as with a weaker vessel" might have been modified to something like "as with a needy vessel" or "as with an insecure vessel."*

> ***TIP:*** *Invite group members to share their thoughts on whether this first exhortation would be stated any differently if it were addressed to wives instead of husbands, and if so, how. Expect some interesting—and possibly humorous—responses here, especially from the wives.*

3. The key word to living successfully with the opposite sex (whether it be a man or woman) is the word, "understanding." Practically, how does one go about obtaining this understanding? What's the process?

4. In order to grasp this first exhortation more fully, let's focus more closely for a moment on the phrase "in an understanding way."

   a. From the original Greek, the phrase is literally translated "according to knowledge." The *King James Version* of the Bible renders it exactly this way.

   b. Further, the word "knowledge" in this literal rendering is often used in reference to the Scriptures.[3]

---

3. W.F. Arndt, and F.W. Gingrich, *A Greek-English Lexicon of the New Testament* (Chicago: University of Chicago Press,1952), p. 163.

Putting these two additional thoughts together, what new insights do you gain from 1 Peter 3:7?

> ***ANSWER:*** *Essentially, the instruction is to love with your mate "according to the insights in Scripture."*

5. On a scale of 1 to 10, how well do you know what the Bible says about marriage, men and women? Please circle one.

1	2	3	4	5	6	7	8	9	10

Very Little   Great
Understanding   Understanding

(This HomeBuilders Couples Series study promises to add points to your score!)

> ***TIP:*** *Comment that if the couples stay with the study and do the **HomeBuilders Projects** each time, they will develop great insights into the differences between men and women and will learn to respond to those differences in healthy, positive ways.*

6. Contrast the "understanding way" being called for by Peter in 1 Peter 3:7 (i.e., the Scripture) with the "way" of Proverbs 16:25 (the way that so many choose in living with their mates). What is this other "way"? Explain.

> ***ANSWER:*** *If we live by our natural instincts, doing what we think is right for us, we are in for trouble. Our natural instincts assume our mate thinks and feels the same way we do. We tend to treat our mate as we want to be treated, which in significant ways can be of a great error. The way that seems right to us*

often does not honor our mate as a unique, special person, and the frequent end result of this path is conflict and abuse.

Lead the group in reading in unison:

HOMEBUILDERS PRINCIPLE #1:

The Scripture will make you wise in the way you live with your mate (Psalm 119:97-100).

C. The Second Exhortation

1. Now notice the second exhortation within 1 Peter 3:7. What major social movement has resulted in part because men have trusted in their natural instincts rather than "the way" encouraged by this Scripture?

    ANSWER: The feminist or women's liberation movement, which has voiced both valid and invalid grievances, can be viewed as a natural reaction to the failure of many husbands to honor their wives as equals and treat them as coheirs in life.

2. Despite their differentness, what "status" does Peter say a husband must always be reaffirming in his wife?

    ANSWER: She is a fellow-heir of all that is good in life and should have an equal share of all that a couple experiences in their marriage.

3. What are some *practical* ways a husband can do this?

> ***TIP:*** *Be prepared to share a few ideas from your experience. After the men have responded, invite the wives to share some things their husbands do now that make them feel honored.*

Call on someone to read aloud:

HOMEBUILDERS PRINCIPLE #2:

True equality in a marriage is achieved when a husband and a wife come to understand, appreciate and honor each other's differentness.

IV. SUMMARY *(1 minute)*

God created unique and special differences in mankind when He created them as male and female. Understanding and responding to these special differences lays a solid foundation upon which to build a strong marriage. This session and the projects which will now follow are presented to help you start this process.

Construction

(to be completed as a couple)
(5-10 minutes)

*This **Construction** section is designed to help a couple begin to interact about ways they can understand and honor their male and female differences.*

Instruct the couples to find a spot where they can talk comfortably (and with some privacy) with each other. Encourage them to keep the focus of their discussion on the positive aspects of their relationship, but also to be willing to consider ways in which they can both grow in understanding one another. Call attention to the personal pledge which both husband and wife should take very seriously. Explain the amount of time they will have to talk about the three items before you call them back for some concluding statements.

Answer the following questions:

1. What areas of our marriage came to mind as a result of tonight's discussion? Why?

2. Wife, what is one thing your husband can do to make you feel more like an equal or coheir? Tell him why this request would be important to you. He needs your feminine perspective to aid his understanding.

3. Conclude your time by reading together the following personal pledge statement:

I pledge to you that I will use the next six weeks of this HomeBuilders study to build, strengthen and encourage our marriage. I will make this study a priority in my schedule by faithfully keeping our "dates," working through the projects and participating in the group discussion. You have my word on it.

   (signed) _____

Will you honor your mate by making this pledge your special commitment to him or her for the coming weeks? If so, sign your name in the space underneath this pledge in **your mate's** study guide to document your commitment.

Make a Date

Each of the seven sessions in this study will end with a **Make a Date**. This is the time you set aside outside each session to do the **HomeBuilders Projects** which you will find at the end of each session. This will be your only homework. Do not begin working on the next session until you meet together again as a group. Do only the assigned **HomeBuilders Project** between sessions.

Now conclude Session One by setting aside one hour in your schedule right now to complete **HomeBuilders Project #1**. As a couple, this project will aid you in continuing the process of building your marriage. Your leader will ask you at the next session to share one thing from this experience.

_____   _____   _____
Date   Time   Location

SPECIAL NOTE: *Save the final minutes to explain the* ***Home-Builders Projects***.

1. *Stress the importance of each couple's setting aside a time between the sessions to talk about the issues that were raised in the previous session. These projects are one of the major keys in gaining real value from this series.*
2. *Share your own experience in doing the projects.*
3. *Point out that the* ***HomeBuilders Project*** *is the only homework before Session Two. (Looking ahead at Session Two is optional.)*
4. *Briefly walk through the* ***HomeBuilders Project*** *for the upcoming week.*

     The individual section should be done by husband and wife separately, as each considers issues from this session. The section to be done as a couple should be done with a positive focus, concentrating on sharing with one another in ways that will be upbuilding.

     Read aloud Ephesians 4:29-32 to emphasize the spirit in which the sharing should be done: seeking mutual insight and understanding rather than airing complaints.
5. *Let group members know they will be held accountable next time to have completed* ***HomeBuilders Project #1***. *Instruct couples to take a minute now to write down the date, time and location when they will meet together. Encourage them to bring their personal or family calendar each week so they can set their date for the coming week.*

Recommended Reading

The books listed at the end of each session are not required, but are recommended to reinforce and expand the concepts dealt with in the group session. Encourage couples to locate this book and read all or part of it before the next session. One effective idea is for one spouse to read aloud to the other, either in the morning before going to work or in the evening before retiring.

Rocking the Roles, by Robert Lewis and William Hendricks.

This book expands upon the content of this study. You'll find it invaluable.

The Art of Understanding Your Mate, by Cecil Osborne.

This book is filled with practical common sense and psychological insights. The author uses many case histories, often humorous, to help husbands and wives better understand each other and build a superior, lasting relationship.

Dismiss in prayer. Mingle with group members after the dismissal, expressing your appreciation for their participation.
Invite everyone to enjoy a time of fellowship and refreshments.

HOMEBUILDERS PROJECT #1

Individually: 15-20 minutes
Write out your answers to the following questions:

1. List two things you want your mate to understand about you that you feel he (or she) is unaware of because of your gender difference.

2. List two things you are having difficulty with in understanding your mate.

3. In what areas have these things affected the quality of your marriage?

4. How can you communicate these things in a way that doesn't attack your mate but instead gives insight and understanding into why these things are important?

Interact as a Couple: 30-45 minutes

1. Read together Ephesians 4:29-32 before beginning your interaction to set the tone of your discussion.

2. Share with your mate your answers to the previous questions.

3. Listen carefully and seek to understand your mate's differentness.

4. Commit to a plan of action that will honor your mate in regard to the things that have been communicated to you. Write out your action plan below. Remember, understanding and responding to male and female differences is important to building a good marriage.

Remember to bring your calendar for **Make a Date**
to the next session.

MEETING YOUR WIFE'S SPECIAL NEEDS

OBJECTIVES

You will help the men in your group to better understand and meet their wives' unique needs as you guide them to:

- List three of the major needs in a woman's life;

- Identify common errors men make in light of women's needs;

- Explore biblical instructions for lovingly meeting a wife's needs; and

- Discuss as a couple specific ways in which the husband has met the wife's needs and practical ideas for improving on those efforts.

OVERALL COMMENTS

The key purpose of this session is to help reveal to each husband what his wife's unique needs are and how he can fulfill those needs. Be aware that in dealing with significant needs, especially those that are not being adequately met, there is great potential for couples to end up merely criticizing each other. Your role as leader is crucial in keeping the session positive and upbeat.

Focus

Women are, by creation, different from men. These differences generate special needs—needs which a husband is uniquely called upon to fulfill.

Warm Up
(10-20 minutes)

1. In Session One, the discussion centered on grappling with those differences which are brought into a marriage by virtue of one partner being male and the other female. What new understanding or fresh insights did you receive in each of the following areas:

Concerning myself I discovered (or was made more aware of)...

Concerning my mate I discovered (or was made more aware of)...

> **TIP:** *Instruct all group members to write down one gender-related insight gained about themselves and one insight about their mate from Session One. After a few moments, invite volunteers to share one insight they wrote down. Be ready to share an insight of your own if needed to stimulate participation.*

2. Would you share from **HomeBuilders Project #1** the action point (or part of it) you wish to take to honor your mate in the weeks to come?

> **TIP:** *Ask for a show of hands of those who completed the **HomeBuilders Project**. Stress that the emphasis of this series is on practical application, not general theories, thus these projects are critical to the impact of the series. Then invite one or two couples to share from their project their plan of action to honor each other's differences.*

(35-45 minutes)

I. WHAT IS IT THAT WOMEN NEED MOST? *(15-20 minutes)*

A. Everyone has needs. Some of these needs, however, are of greater importance to women than they are to men. Wives: Share what you believe these special feminine needs are. Then discuss which of these needs are the three greatest. Husbands: Listen carefully! Everyone: Take notes!

Our top three choices are:

   1.

   2.

   3.

B. Colossians 3:19 says, "Husbands, love your wives, and do not be embittered against them." This verse has something special to say about a woman's needs. By way of a command it urges husbands to be active in meeting what the Bible considers the most important need a wife possesses. What is that need? How does it compare with the wives "choices" of greatest needs?

> ***ANSWER:*** *Love. In all likelihood, most of the top choices the women list will be practical expressions of the basic need for love.*
>
> ***TIP:*** *Call on one woman to read aloud Colossians 3:19, which urges husbands to meet what the Bible considers the most important need a wife possesses.*

Conclude this discussion by pointing out that this session will focus on one key need of a woman, the need to be loved rightly! Rightly is the key word. A man may love his wife and his dog, but he loves them differently. A wife needs to be loved, not just differently, but rightly. Before looking at what Scripture spells out about the specifics of how to show love rightly, it is helpful to see some common mistakes—"Where Husbands Sometimes Go Wrong."

II. WHERE HUSBANDS SOMETIMES GO WRONG *(5 minutes)*

Notice the contrasting phrase of Colossians 3:19. The word translated "embittered" means "to be exasperated" with.[1] It suggests a growing and deepening frustration, irritation and anger with one's wife.

Husbands: We sometimes become "embittered" with our wives because we don't understand them. Think carefully here. In

---

1. H.G. Liddell, and Scott, *Greek-English Lexicon* (Oxford: Clarendon Press, 1975), p. 639.

what areas have you at times detected a *growing* resentment or exasperation with your wife which short-circuits the expression of your love she so needs? List one or two examples below.

Remember that your wife as a female goes about things differently than you do as a male. Remember too, Peter's admonition: "Husbands...live with your wives in an understanding way" (1 Peter 3:7).

> **TIP:** *Share one way in which you have detected a resentment or exasperation with your wife which short-circuits the expression of your love she so needs. Invite volunteers to share their own experiences. If the men are reluctant to open up, ask each wife to suggest one area in which her husband becomes irritated with her. Point out that all couples face the problem of exasperating each other.*
>
> *Comment that sometimes a husband feels frustration or anger because he is misunderstanding his wife as a female. Call attention to the instruction in 1 Peter 3:7 to "live with your wives in an understanding way."*

III. How to Love Your Wife
Rightly (15-20 minutes)

Let's explore this basic need for love more closely. Certainly the word "love" means different things to different people. But in marriage, the Bible says that the love a woman needs is something *very specific*. Review this more specific description of love in Ephesians 5:25-29. We will focus on three particular qualities that define the kind of love a wife needs.

A. The First Quality

1. The first specific quality defining a husband's love for his wife is found in verse 25 with the comparison of Christ's love for the church. What characteristic of love stands out in this comparison?

   ANSWER: *Sacrifice marks the first characteristic needed in a husband's love. This is the same sacrifice that Christ made when He gave Himself up for His church.*

2. In order for Christ to love the church the way He did, who did He often have to say no to? (For help, see also Philippians 2:3-5 and Matthew 20:28.)

   ANSWER: *Himself*

   TIP: *Call on someone in the group to read aloud Philippians 2:3-5.*

3. When a man responds to a woman in this way, what does this kind of love say to her?

   ANSWER: *He is saying to her that she is very important and valuable, affirming her great worth. That affirmation of worth meets a great need in a woman. Thus, the first quality needed in a husband's love is his sacrificial declaration of her importance and worth.*

B. The Second Quality

1. A second specific quality defining a husband's love for his wife is found within verses 27-28a. How do these verses suggest that a husband's love should specifically promote, develop and enhance his wife's life?

ANSWER: What we see in verse 27 is Christ trying to present His church with no blemish at all. To that end, He has lived for her so that the church will develop and blossom "in all her glory." His goal is to produce a church that will become truly glorious. In the same way, a husband is to live for his wife in such a way that she might blossom into all that she was meant to be. The husband is to encourage his wife, assisting her to grow into full use of her God-given potential. A second quality of a husband's love is encouragement of her development.

What key words stand out in verse 27 in this regard? For instance, how would you practically define the phrase "in all her glory" as far as a wife is concerned?

ANSWER: The husband cannot try to make his wife into what he wants her to be; he is to aid her in becoming all that she was meant to be. He is to live for her so that her glory as a woman might show.

2. How could these verses be used to address the low self-esteem problem and inferior feelings that so often plague a woman's life?[2] (A review of letters C and F under "Practical Differences" in Session One might be helpful in answering this question.)

---

2. As reported in James Dobson's book, *What Wives Wish Their Husbands Knew About Women* (Wheaton: Tyndale House Publishers, 1986), pp. 22-41. Note the following excerpt: "If I could write a prescription for the women of the world, I would provide each one of them with a healthy dose of self-esteem and personal worth (taken three times a day until the symptoms disappear). I have no doubt that this is their greatest need . . . if they felt equal with men in personal worth, they would not need to be equivalent to men in responsibility. If they could only bask in the dignity and status granted them by the Creator, then their femininity would be valued as their greatest asset, rather than scorned as an old garment to be discarded. Without question, the future of a nation depends on how it sees its women, and I hope we will teach our little girls to be glad they were chosen by God for the special pleasures of womanhood" (p. 35).

> **ANSWER:** *A husband who builds up his wife, helping her to grow to her full capabilities, will allow her to escape the feelings of inferiority that plague so many women. Read aloud the quote by James Dobson found in the footnote. When a man affirms his wife and encourages her by stressing her importance to him, then she is far less likely to feel inferior and more likely to have the confidence to grow and mature.*

3. What is the blueprint a husband should follow in seeking his wife's best (see v. 26)?

> **ANSWER:** *He should encourage her spiritual growth, following biblical guidelines.*

C. The Third Quality

1. A final specific quality that should mark a husband's love for his wife is found in verses 28b-29. Two important and positive "action" words mark out this final aspect of love in verse 29. Fill in the blanks below with these two critical verbs:

_____ meaning "to provide for"

and

_____ meaning "to protect and take care of"

A helpful insight into this second word comes from its usage to describe "birds covering their young with their feathers."[3] The need for security is one of the strongest emotional needs a woman possesses."[4]

---

3. W.E. Vine, *Expository Dictionary of New Testament Words* (Old Tappan, NJ: Fleming H. Revell Co., 1966), p. 184.

4. Cecil Osborne, *The Art of Understanding Your Mate* (Grand Rapids: Zondervan Publishing House, 1977), p. 50.

> ***ANSWER:*** *"Nourish," meaning "to provide for," and "cherish," meaning "to protect and take care of." The third quality of a husband's love is provision of strong security.*

2. Husbands: Discuss several practical ways you as a husband can love your wife by nourishing and cherishing her.

> ***TIP:*** *Be prepared with a few thoughts of your own in response to number 2.*

3. Wives: What helpful suggestions would you offer?

> ***TIP:*** *Ask the wives for any helpful suggestions they could offer the men for actions that would help them feel more secure. Keep the emphasis positive here, avoiding statements of criticism or complaints of any lapses in the past.*

IV. SUMMARY *(1 minute)*

Through her husband a woman's special need of love is to be fulfilled. His love for her should be the kind that specifically (1) declares her importance and worth, (2) seeks her personal development, and (3) provides for her a strong sense of security. Nothing less will do.

TIP: *Read aloud the summary statement and instruct everyone to underline each of the three qualities of love mentioned in the paragraph.*

Construction

(to be completed as a couple)
(5-10 minutes)

*This **Construction** section will help couples talk with each other about ways in which the husband communicates his love to his wife.*

Guide the couples to places where they can have some privacy to talk together. Explain that at the end of the time, you will call the group back together for some final directions to conclude this session.

1. Wives, write down two things your husband has done (or is doing) that make you feel loved and for which you are most grateful.

2. Husbands, write down one practical area you could improve in so that your wife could more fully see your love for her. "Husbands ought...to love their own wives as their own bodies" (v. 28).

3. Share your conclusions with one another.

> *TIP: Instruct the wives to share their responses to Question 1 before the husbands share their responses to Question 2. Encourage the wives to be positive and encouraging to help their husbands see ways they have rightly loved their wives.*

HOMEBUILDERS PRINCIPLE #3:

The greatest need a woman has in her marriage is to be loved rightly.

Call time and instruct the couples to take a few moments to pray together before they regather for the session conclusion. Encourage them to thank God both for each other and for the qualities each one shows which communicate love.

*Regather the group and call attention to **HomeBuilders Principle #3**, stressing the word "rightly."*

Make a Date

*Introduce **HomeBuilders Project #2**, pointing out that the husband should spend time reviewing this session, focusing on a woman's needs. At the same time the wife needs to evaluate how she feels about her husband's love for her. This can be potentially volatile, so urge the wives to be thoughtful and gentle when sharing their responses. Encourage couples to keep looking for positive solutions, again using Ephesians 4:29-32 as a backdrop for their interaction together.*

Make a date with your mate to meet in the next few days to complete **HomeBuilders Project #2**.

| Date | Time | Location |

Instruct couples to set the time they will meet this week to complete the project.

Recommended Reading

(for husbands only)

What Wives Wish Their Husbands Knew About Women, by James Dobson.

In this classic best-seller, Dobson identifies the 10 main causes of dissatisfaction and unhappiness among women in the marriage relationship.

Point out the reading suggestion for men who wish to understand and love their wives more fully.

Dismiss in prayer and engage group members in friendly conversation over some light refreshments.

HomeBuilders Project #2

Individually: 15-20 minutes

1. Husband: Carefully review Session Two.

2. Wife: Complete the following project, circling the numbers that apply and filling in the blanks:

Because of my husband's love...

a. I feel extremely valuable.

1	2	3	4	5	6	7	8	9	10
Rarely				Some of the time					Always

Please explain:

If there are problems here, your suggested solution:

b. I feel I am becoming all God meant for me to be.

1	2	3	4	5	6	7	8	9	10

Rarely   Some of the time   Always

Please explain:

If there are problems here, your suggested solution:

c. I feel secure, protected and provided for.

1	2	3	4	5	6	7	8	9	10

Rarely   Some of the time   Always

Please explain:

If there are problems here, your suggested solution:

Interact as a Couple: 45 minutes

1. Begin by reading Ephesians 4:29-32 together.

2. Wives: Share your completed project with your husband in a way that makes no demands but which promotes positive communication about your three areas of need.

3. Decide together which of these three areas needs the most immediate attention. Then decide on one practical step that you as a husband can take *now* to better meet this need.

Please be sure you agree on this action step and how it will be implemented.

4. Close your time in prayer, committing this action step to the Lord.

Remember to bring your calendar for **Make a Date** to the next session.

MEETING YOUR HUSBAND'S SPECIAL NEEDS

OBJECTIVES

You will help the women in your group to better understand and meet their husbands' unique needs as you guide them to:

- List three of the major needs in a man's life;
- Discover what Scripture says a husband needs most from his wife;
- Explore biblical instructions for three ways a wife can meet a husband's needs; and
- Discuss as a couple specific ways in which the wife has met the husband's needs and practical ideas for improving in those efforts.

OVERALL COMMENTS

This session seeks to reveal to the women what a man's unique needs are and how a wife can fulfill those needs. Many wives have spent considerable time in their marriages dealing with their husband's needs. Be prepared for some who feel—even after the past week—that they have carried an unfair load in meeting their husband's needs while not having their own met. They may need patient help in seeing that unselfishly meeting the needs of their mate is often the means by which their mate becomes able to reciprocate.

Focus

Men are, by creation, different from women. These differences generate special needs—needs which a wife is uniquely called upon to fulfill.

Warm Up

(10-20 minutes)

1. Husbands, from your time on **HomeBuilders Project #2**, share one specific way you've chosen to love your wife differently than before.

> **TIP:** *Ask for a show of hands of those who completed the past session's **HomeBuilders Project**. Remind the group that the focus of this series is on practical application at home, not on the discussions with the group. Invite two or three husbands to share from their project the step they have agreed upon to love their wives differently than before, so that they can better meet their wives' needs.*

2. What is the most significant insight you have gained so far concerning men, women, their differences and marriage?

(35-45 minutes)

I. WHAT IS IT THAT MEN NEED MOST?
(10-15 minutes)

In Session Two the wives were given the opportunity to discuss their needs as women. Now it's the husbands' turns. Husbands: What do you think are your special needs as a man? Record helpful comments below, then see if some general agreement can be found by the men as to your three greatest needs. Wives: Listen carefully. Everyone: Take notes.

Our Top Three Choices Are:

1.

2.

3.

II. WHAT THE BIBLE HAS TO SAY
(15-20 minutes)

A. The Major Needs of Women and Men

The Scripture reveals that what a man needs most from a woman in marriage is strikingly different from what a woman needs most from a man. In the last session, Paul's letter to the Ephesians helped us see what a wife needs from her husband. It can be summed up in one word:

_____ (Ephesians 5:25)

ANSWER: *Love*

In this same chapter, another single word sums up what a husband consistently needs from his wife. Read Ephesians 5:33 and record this key word which Paul selects:

> ***ANSWER:*** *Respect.*
>
> ***TIP:*** *Point out that, just as love has specific aspects to it, so this word respect has different aspects as well. That will be the focus of the exploration in this session. Expect that some men may not immediately identify their need for respect, but as they hear how that word is lived out by a wife, they will become more aware of its great value to their total well-being as men.*

B. The Importance of Respect to a Man

Many men are not aware of how important respect is to them. Some women may not be aware of it either. Before going further, let's brainstorm over what this word respect actually means. What other words come to mind when you think of this word "respect"? A dictionary definition might be a helpful place to begin.

Now put some additional "color" into this word by thinking of it in terms of a wife's responsiveness to her husband. What would respect look like to you in the everyday of a marriage relationship?

> ***TIP:*** *Ask, "What specific actions by a wife would communicate respect to you?"*

However a man may appear, his nature is basically insecure. Often a man's masculinity is more fragile than a woman's femininity...his self-esteem is more easily threatened. Men, more than women, have a need to "prove" themselves, for doubts are always lingering. The view a man has of himself (whether good or bad) is usually a reflection from two sources: his work and his woman. If either of these become shaky, so do his feelings and perceptions about his manhood. Depression and anger often fill such times. A wife's ongoing responsiveness to her husband should be a well from which a husband can draw respect for himself. His self-respect is, in many ways, her respect reborn in him.

> ***TIP:*** *Invite the wives to respond to the paragraph, "How does this paragraph make you feel about the importance of a wife's communicating respect to her husband?" If the major needs the men listed earlier in the session do not reveal awareness of insecurity, you may need to stress the importance of a wife's being able to recognize many of the typical male behaviors which are consciously or unconsciously intended to mask inner fears and concerns. Be prepared to share some of your own insecurities if you sense any of the wives (or their husbands) have not fully accepted the need for respect as crucial to a husband's well-being.*

III. THREE VALUABLE WAYS A WIFE CAN RESPECT HER HUSBAND
(10-15 minutes)

A. By Honoring and Esteeming Him

1. How does Proverbs 12:4 picture the impact a wife can have on her husband?

ANSWER: Proverbs 12:4 pictures an excellent wife as "the crown of her husband."

TIP: Focus on this positive imagery, but be aware that the latter half of the verse depicts the opposite of admiration—action that shames him, makes him feel worthless. This aspect of the verse will be dealt with in Item 5.

2. What does a crown signify? How would wearing a crown suddenly change the perception others had of you? How would it raise your own self-perception?

ANSWER: Obviously, wearing a crown makes someone look more important to others and gives added confidence to the person wearing it. A wife raises her husband's own esteem of himself by honoring him. She makes him feel better about himself and what he does.

3. Paul uses this same figure in expressing his feelings about the believers in Thessalonica. They were his "crown." What words did Paul use in 1 Thessalonians 2:19-20 to describe the impact these believers had on his life?

ANSWER: Glory and joy—and that is what a wife becomes to her husband. By her life with him, she gives to him glory and joy and hope, making him feel better about himself.

These same words would apply when a wife is the "crown" of her husband.

4. Husbands: List one or two occasions in which your wife has been like a crown to you. Describe your feelings on such occasions.

5. Look back at Proverbs 12:4. Although this verse says a wife can be like a crown to her husband, it also indicates that a wife also possesses the power to "shame" her husband. The phrase "shames him" speaks of disrespect or public embarrassment. It has overtones of making one either feel or become worthless.[1] What are some ways women can undercut their husbands, making them feel worthless or embarrassed? Publicly? Privately?

Husbands: You will need to take the lead in helping to answer this question.

> **ANSWER:** *A common illustration of this occurs if a man is talking to someone else about his job (or any other topic his wife has heard about repeatedly), and his wife looks bored, rolls her eyeballs, or in other ways communicates that what he says is not important to her. This is likely to produce anger at being belittled. Also, disagreeing with her husband is a typical way a wife communicates a disparaging view of his value.*
>
> **TIP:** *Call attention to the contrasting phrase of Proverbs 12:4 which indicates that while a wife can be like a crown to her husband, she also possesses the power to shame her husband.*
> *Be very clear in your directions so that men do not share about their own wives, but that the exam-*

---

1. *Nelson's Expository Dictionary of the Old Testament* (Nashville: Thomas Nelson Publishers, 1980), p. 371.

ples mentioned are dealing only with ways other women sometimes shame their husbands. Be prepared with a few examples of your own if needed to make sure that the wives understand that it is very easy literally to destroy a man's self-esteem in public by things that they say or in ways that they act.

6. Wives: What gracious "words of praise" would your husband love to hear from you that would honor him and give him a greater sense of his value as a man? (See Proverbs 16:24.) List some below.

> **TIP:** *Call on one of the wives to read aloud Proverbs 16:24, keeping her finger in Proverbs 12:4. Point out the contrast in terms between the two verses ("sweet to the soul and healing to the bones" vs. "rottenness in his bones").*
>
> *Summarize this sharing by restating that by honoring and esteeming her husband, a wife demonstrates the respect that he desperately needs in order to be a healthy, growing man, able to carry out his responsibilities in life.*

B. By Supporting (and Not Competing with) Him

1. Notice the support the "excellent wife" of Proverbs 31:10-12 gives to her husband. What specific insights about her are revealed in these verses?

> **ANSWER:** *Her worth is above jewels, she is trustworthy, she brings her husband gain and good, not evil.*
>
> **TIP:** *Call on a woman to read aloud Proverbs 31:10-12.*

2. What does Proverbs 21:9,19 say about a wife who competes with her husband?

> *TIP: Call on another woman to read aloud Proverbs 21:9,19. Invite comments from the group about a "contentious woman"—a wife who competes with her husband. Ask, "How does that make a husband feel about himself? About her?"*

3. Husbands: Share one area of your life where your wife's support directly contributed to your success. Be sure to include *how* and *why* it did so.

> *TIP: Be prepared to share an incident from your own marriage to help stimulate interaction.*

4. Wives: In what specific area could your husbands use more support from you? How could your active support (rather than passivity, criticism, inflexibility, resistance, etc.) make a difference?

> *TIP: Ask the women why that demonstration of active support could make a difference in a man's life. Summarize the idea-sharing by reminding the group that their ideas are illustrations of practical ways in which a wife shows respect for her husband.*

C. By Physically Responding to Him

Few areas affirm a man *as a man* as does his wife's sexual responsiveness to him. Spontaneous hugs and kisses or other demonstrations of affection, as well as lovemaking, all do more than just give pleasure. These things reassure a man— they confirm him in his masculinity.

1. Notice as an example the responsiveness of the Shulamite bride to Solomon (Song of Solomon 7:10-12). Husbands: How would you feel at such words? How does this communicate respect?

     TIP: Call on one of the men to read aloud Song of Solomon 7:10-12.

2. Husbands: How has your wife's physical responsiveness positively affected your view of yourself? Explain.

     TIP: Encourage the men to express for the wives' benefit how their view of themselves as men is affected by their wife's positive physical responsiveness.

     Call on one of the wives to read aloud.

HOMEBUILDERS PRINCIPLE #4:

Other than a man's relationship with the Lord, few things tell a man more about himself than does the respect of his wife.

IV. SUMMARY *(1 minute)*

A respectful wife is life-giving to a man. He draws from her a strong and affirmative sense of who he is. Clearly a wife can brighten her husband's life by her admiration and esteem. She can stabilize his life by her supportiveness. She can also energize his life by her physical responsiveness. In short, she is called to fulfill many of his deepest needs through the simple admonition: "See to it that you respect your husband." (See Ephesians 5:33.)

Construction

(to be completed as a couple)
(5-10 minutes)

*This **Construction** section is an imposing-looking activity, but each couple focuses only on the section of the Adult Male Life Cycle chart which currently applies. They then talk together about ways a woman's respect could help a man during that stage of life, applying insights gained during the session.*

Instruct couples to move to a private place where they can talk openly with each other. Alert them that this project touches on some potentially sensitive issues. Explain that they only need to concern themselves with one section of the Life Cycle chart. State the time at which you will regather the group to conclude the session. Instruct them to conclude their project with a brief prayer for each other before they return to the group.

There has been much research in the area of adult male development. It has been documented that all men have a common pattern underlying their lives.[2] Each man's adult life consists at points called "transitions," meaning that as one stage is ending, a new one is getting underway.

1. Separately look over the Adult Male Life Cycle charted on the pages that follow.

2. Focus on that stage which is relevant to you as a man (and to you as a couple).

3. In the space provided on the right side of the chart, list practical ways a wife's respect (as defined in this session) would cause her husband to succeed in that particular stage of his life with its unique pressures and stresses.

4. Share your feelings and conclusions with one another after you have recorded your thoughts.

5. If you find you need more interaction time, then begin the **HomeBuilders Project** by finishing up any incomplete discussion.

---

2. Material adapted here is based on the extensive research done by Daniel Levinson and published in his book, *Seasons of a Man's Life* (New York: Ballantine Books), 1978.

ADULT MALE LIFE CYCLE

Early Adulthood —— Middle Adulthood —— Late Adulthood					
	Early to Middle Adult Transition		Middle to Late Adult Transition		

Age 20   40   45   60   65   + +

CHARACTERISTICS OF STAGES AND TRANSITIONS

Stage	Characteristics	How a Woman's Respect Helps...
Early Adulthood (20-40)	Struggle to establish self in society... *Starting* is the key word (job, marriage, family, home, etc.). A time for men to dream. A time of stress, doubt and insecurity. Usually a stressful vocational move is made around 30 as a man seeks to position himself for the future.	
Early to Middle Adult Transition (40-45)	Major turning point as life shifts from youth to middle age. Temptation to reclaim neglected parts of youth stage which now seek expression (sometimes urgently). A pivotal period of inner evaluation, psychologically stressful...appraising self in relation to job, marriage, meaning, etc. Must come to terms with questions such as: What have I done?; Where am I now?; Of what value is my life...to others, to society, to me? This period can produce extreme crisis and even panic behavior...the infamous midlife crisis.	

Stage	Characteristics	How a Woman's Respect Helps...
Middle Adulthood (45-60)	Based upon the previous transition, a sense of a new beginning or a growing sense of regression, stagnation, or even failure. Distinct sense of bodily decline and the passing away of youth. Ever-growing sense of mortality. The quality and character of the rest of a man's life is usually determined here.	
Middle to Late Adulthood Transition (60-65)	Decreasing vigor and capacity; coming to terms with what this now means. Moving off center stage can be traumatic to some—less recognition, authority and power. Who am I now?—deep struggle of reappraisal.	
Late Adulthood (65+)	Retirement...a time of satisfaction and serenity or bitterness, disappointment, resentment and fear. A time closely connected to the decisions and events of middle adulthood. What can I do now?	

Make a Date

This session's **HomeBuilders Project** *mirrors last session's. The wife reviews the session while the husband completes the evaluation project. He then shares his feelings about his wife's respect, focusing on positive actions she could take to help and respect him better in specific areas. Again, this sharing needs to grow out of Ephesians 4:29-32 so that it remains upbeat and constructive, not loaded with criticism and complaint.*

Make a date with your mate to meet in the next few days to complete **HomeBuilders Project #3**.

Date	Time	Location

Instruct couples to mark on the calendars the time they will set aside in the coming weeks to meet together to complete this project. Encourage the couples to keep making these projects a priority, giving them quality time. This will enhance their marriage far beyond what they gain from these sessions.

Recommended Reading

(for wives)

Creative Counterpart, by Linda Dillow.

A creative counterpart is more than just a helper. She is a woman who, having chosen a vocation of wife and mother, decides to learn and grow in all the areas of this role. Linda Dillow tells how to become such a person in this unique book that is entertaining, practical and biblically based.

Dismiss the session in prayer and take time for informal interaction and refreshments with the group members.

HOMEBUILDERS PROJECT #3

Individually: 10-15 minutes

1. Wife: Review carefully Session Three.

2. Husband: Complete the following project, circling the numbers that apply and filling in the blanks.

Because of my wife's respect...

a. I feel honored and esteemed as a man.

1	2	3	4	5	6	7	8	9	10

Rarely   Some of the time   Always

Please explain:

If there are problems here, your suggested solution:

b. I feel supported and encouraged as a man.

1	2	3	4	5	6	7	8	9	10

Rarely   Some of the time   Always

Please explain:

If there are problems here, your suggested solution:

c. I feel physically affirmed as a man.

1	2	3	4	5	6	7	8	9	10

Rarely   Some of the time   Always

Please explain:

If there are problems here, your suggested solution:

Interact as a Couple: 25-30 minutes

1. Begin by reading **again** Ephesians 4:29-32.

2. Husbands: Share your completed project with your wife in a way that makes no demands but which promotes clear communication about your three areas of need.

3. Decide together which of these three areas needs the most immediate attention. Wives: Discuss with your husband one practical step you can take now to better meet this need.

Please be sure you agree on this action step and how it will be implemented.

4. Close your time in prayer, committing this action to the Lord.

Remember to bring your calendar for **Make a Date**
to the next session.

ROLE RESPONSIBILITIES FOR THE MAN

OBJECTIVES

You will help your group accurately define the husband's core role in marriage as you lead the group to:

- Evaluate experiences which have influenced their view of a man's role in marriage;
- Distinguish between a core role and comprehensive life-styles;
- Examine scriptural instructions about a man's role in marriage; and
- Consider how a man can apply his scriptural responsibilities in today's society.

OVERALL COMMENTS

1. This session focuses on accurately defining the husband's core role in marriage. Note the important distinction between a core role and comprehensive life-styles or specific tasks. The core role is defined as central to a marriage, but not covering everything that person does as a marriage partner.

2. Spend some time before the session thinking through how to honor the requirements of a core role while allowing latitude, creativity and flexibility in the totality of a man's life. The decision about whether the husband or wife will fix breakfast or wash the car is not necessarily related to either person's core role in the marriage, but is often a matter of personal preference, skills, schedules, or other factors which vary widely from couple to couple. The core roles assigned by Scripture, however, apply to all marriages which seek to fulfill God's purposes.

3. Try to keep attention focused on the issue of core roles, guiding people to defer consideration of specific job functions.

Focus

The Bible sets forth specific roles
for men and women in marriage.
Any couple serious about pleasing
God will seek to shape their
marriage around these general role
responsibilities. For the man,
the divine challenge is to be
a servant-leader.

Warm Up

(5-10 minutes)

*This **Warm Up** is intended to continue building relationships among group members while introducing them to the topic of leadership.*

*Your personal interest and acceptance is crucial in helping people feel positive about tackling the difficult issues raised in this session. Ask for a show of hands of those who completed **HomeBuilders Project #3**. Commend those who did so for keeping their commitment to building their marriages.*

1. Privately, list three leaders whom you have come to admire greatly. In your mind, what made them both great and effective?

2. Share your conclusions with the rest of the group.

> *TIP: Instruct everyone to list on their study guide page all the qualities people mention. When the list is complete, guide the group in selecting those qualities that seem most significant.*

3. What are the qualities that made Jesus a great leader? What qualities seem to stand out above the rest? Record the group's insights in the space below.

> *TIP: Point out that, as you progress in this session, you will be exploring the concept of leadership in relationship to a man's role as husband. However, before looking at any specific roles, it is important to get an overall perspective on roles within a marriage.*

(40-60 minutes)

I. AN OVERALL PERSPECTIVE ON ROLES
(10-20 minutes)

A. There Are No Role-less Marriages.
In time, every marriage will settle into some social and organizational arrangement causing both husband and wife to play specific roles which uphold it. What structure a couple ultimately decides upon depends upon which "voices" they consider authoritative. Review the list of voices below that are so powerfully influential in the structuring of a marriage

and the roles people play. Rank them 1-6, using number 1 to represent the *most* influential authority behind your own marriage and number 6 as the *least* influential one.

_____ How I saw my parents live out their marriage

_____ What I have "absorbed" from today's culture

_____ How my peers have chosen to live out their marriages

_____ The Bible

_____ What I have read in books, studied, seen, etc.

_____ Other sources:_____

> **TIP:** *Point out that while this session will focus on the husband's role in marriage, you will begin by looking at roles in general. The issue of roles in marriage is a very volatile subject, with people taking strong stands in favor of or opposition to certain roles for husbands and wives.*
>
> *Call attention to the statement: There are no roleless marriages. Stress that every married couple lives out roles in their relationship to one another, to their children and to others whom they contact. In every marriage there have been and continue to be many factors which influence the roles adopted by the husband and wife.*
>
> *Instruct each person, working privately, to rank the factors listed in the study guide in order of their relative influence on the roles in the marriage. (Number 1 represents the most influential authority and number 6 is the least influential one.)*

1. Compare your list with your spouse's list.

> **TIP:** *After a few minutes, instruct everyone to compare their list with their spouse's list—just for fun!*

2. Share with the group which "voice" has influenced your marriage the most. The least? Explain.

3. What warning does Psalm 127:1 give to any couple regarding the structure of their marriage?

> **ANSWER:** *Unless the Lord builds—structures—the house, all building effort is in vain.*
>
> *Summarize this opening discussion by emphasizing that while we are all influenced by a variety of factors in our lives, it is crucial that the roles we adopt are those the Lord intends, not those recommended by any other source.*

B. A Very Important Announcement

There is great misunderstanding concerning the roles of men and women today. Therefore, it is extremely important that you not jump to conclusions about what a session will teach beforehand. The titles selected for a husband's role and a wife's role in the next session should be considered as core roles and not comprehensive life-styles. In other words, these roles for husbands and wives, though essential to a marriage, are not all one does in the marriage. It would be a great mistake, for instance, to conclude that the role label "helper-homemaker" in Session Five is meant to imply that all a woman does is stay at home and submit to her husband. This is an understandable reaction in light of our culture, but unfair and inaccurate to the truth soon to be addressed in these sessions. There is great latitude, creativity and flexibility around one's core role. There is also great danger in ignoring these core roles, altering them, or violating them. Throughout the next two sessions, you will do well to remember this word "core" as opposed to comprehensive. We are addressing the core structure of your marriage, not the entire life-style of a man or a woman.

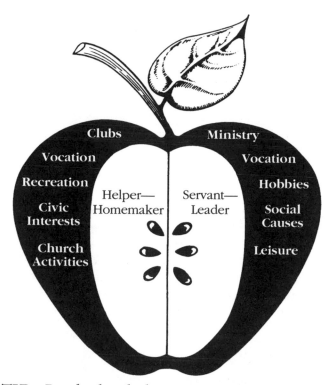

TIP: *Read aloud the paragraph headed "A Very Important Announcement." Make sure your group understands that this session and the one following deal with core roles, not comprehensive life-styles or specific tasks. These sessions will explore the biblical teaching that the husband's core role is to be a servant-leader while the wife's core role is shown to be helper-homemaker. These are never presented as describing the totality of a person's life, but as a central focus around which a person may build varied interests and involvements. All other forms of employment, recreation and ministry will naturally vary in intensity and importance in different stages of life. At no time, however, can husband or wife allow any other enterprise to infringe upon or usurp his or her core role. By stressing both mutual responsibility to the core roles and flexibility and creativity in building a life-style around them, you will help partici-*

pants get over the emotional threat and misunder-
standing that some will bring to this topic. It is crucial
to avoid the common errors of either throwing out the
biblical roles or forcing people to limit themselves
totally within those roles. While people may have
many questions and misgivings at this point, assure
them that God's intent for their marriage is always
for their benefit. The core roles are best because they
are part of God's perfect design.

II. GOD'S CORE ROLE FOR HUSBANDS
(15-20 minutes)

"For the husband is the head of the wife, as Christ also is the
head of the church, He Himself being the Savior of the body"
(Ephesians 5:23).

> **TIP:** *Instruct everyone to read Ephesians 5:23 silently.*

A. Misunderstandings of Headship

1. What is your present understanding of Paul's statement, "the
   husband is the head of the wife?"[1] Does the thought of "privilege" or "responsibility" first come to mind? What feelings
   surface with this statement?

2. Historically, it should be noted that Paul's statement in Ephesians 5:23 is not drawn from a culture where men reigned
   unchallenged as heads of their women. In fact, a serious
   breakdown of marriage and family was occurring throughout
   the Roman Empire at this time. Both men and women were
   resisting the idea that a man was the head of his wife, but for
   different reasons. Men really did not want the responsibility;

---

1. The word for "head" is to be understood in a figurative sense denoting "leadership of" or
   "having authority over." For a deeper study of the word "head" see the fine discussion of it in
   James B. Hurley's book, *Man and Woman in Biblical Perspective* (Grand Rapids: Zondervan
   Publishing House, 1981), pp. 144-145, 163-168.

women were increasingly reluctant to give up their rights. Therefore, Paul's call for a man to be the head of his wife sounded as radical to many then as it does to many now. See 1 Corinthians 11:2,3. Notice that the Corinthians held firmly to all Paul's teaching (v. 2) but obviously struggled over the understanding of headship (v. 3).

TIP: Call on a man to read aloud the historical statement about the role of husbands in Paul's society. Invite a volunteer to read aloud 1 Corinthians 11:2,3.

3. What dangers or misunderstandings are inherent in the concept of male headship?

HOMEBUILDERS PRINCIPLE #5:

It is crucial that a husband's leadership role be accurately defined before it can be accurately fulfilled.

The next section provides this definition by giving a helpful comparison of leadership in the home with Jesus' leadership in the church.

B. Clarifying the Husband's Leadership Role

1. Notice again Ephesians 5:23. With whom is the husband's leadership style to be compared?

ANSWER: Christ.

2. Contrasting Leadership Styles

   a. How did Jesus express His leadership style in Luke 22:25-27 and Matthew 20:25-28?

   And He said to them, "The kings of the Gentiles lord it over them; and those who have authority over them are called 'Benefactors.' But not so with you, but let him who is the greatest among you become as the youngest, and the leader as the servant. For who is greater, the one who reclines at the table, or the one who serves? Is it not the one who reclines at the table? But I am among you as the one who serves" (Luke 22:25-27).

   But Jesus called them to Himself, and said, "You know that the rulers of the Gentiles lord it over them, and their great men exercise authority over them. It is not so among you, but whoever wishes to become great among you shall be your servant, and whoever wishes to be first among you shall be your slave; just as the Son of Man did not come to be served, but to serve, and to give His life a ransom for many" (Matthew 20:25-28).

   ANSWER: *Servant, one who gives.*

   b. Describe the Gentile leadership style represented in these passages. What key words found in these verses give this kind of leadership its "flavor"?

   ANSWER: *The key words which give this kind of leadership its "flavor" are "lord it over" and "exercise authority." In today's world the words are "control," "boss," and "manipulate." The Gentile leader sees himself in the position where he is to receive benefit—work, service, loyalty, etc., from those he leads.*
   Expect some men to have difficulty reconciling

serving with leading. You may need to state several times that almost everything in our society conditions us to view these terms as opposites. Jesus was truly revolutionary when He linked them together, defining leadership as service and service as leadership.

3. Against which of these two leadership styles are women most reacting today?

4. Using the chart on the following page, contrast the way a serving leader and a lording leader would handle everyday situations with his wife. Be specific.

> **TIP:** *As you guide the group in completing the chart, stress the need to be specific, as in the example given of making a major purchase.*

The Lording Leader	Situation	The Serving Leader
Example: Buys what pleases ← him. Is impulsive. Does not ask for or take into consideration his wife's insight on such a purchase. Overlooks her needs and the needs of his family.	Making a major purchase.	*Example:* → Deliberates with his wife before making such a decision. Is considerate of her feelings. Exalts the needs of his wife and family above his own.
←	Responsibilities around the home.	→
←	Disciplining the children.	→
←	Arriving at a difficult decision.	→
←	Listening to his wife's suggestions.	→
←	Handling finances.	→
←	Spiritual initiatives: prayer, church, Bible study, etc.	→
←	Scheduling.	→

III. THREE LEADERSHIP RESPONSIBILITIES FOR SERVANT-LEADERS *(10-15 minutes)*

Complete the following statements in your own words by reading the passages of Scripture associated with them. Discuss what each of these statements would look like in the everyday of a marriage. Then list practical suggestions a man could take to enhance his leadership performance in each area:

"He must be one who manages his own household well, keeping his children under control with all dignity" (1 Timothy 3:4).

A. A servant-leader will _____ his household well.

Practical ideas:

> **ANSWER:** *Manage.*

"And, fathers, do not provoke your children to anger; but bring them up in the discipline and instruction of the Lord" (Ephesians 6:4; see also Deuteronomy 6:6-7).

B. A servant-leader will _____ his children.

Practical ideas:

> **ANSWER:** *Discipline and spiritually instruct.*

"Do not merely look out for your own personal interests, but also for the interests of others. Have this attitude in yourselves which was also in Christ Jesus" (Philippians 2:4,5).

C. A servant-leader will _____ his wife.

Practical ideas:

> **ANSWER:** *Look out for the interests of others.*

> **TIP:** *Invite people to share examples that they've observed in homes.*

IV. PERSPECTIVES FOR WIVES
(10-15 minutes)

A. The Wife Is Subject to Her Husband

1. This session has focused on the role of a husband as a leader. But what implications are there for the wife in this regard? Read again Ephesians 5:22-24, this time spotlighting the two verses that come before and after verse 23. What do these verses say about a wife's responsiveness?

2. Wives: How does clarifying and defining the man's core role make the thought of submission easier and more reasonable?

3. Husbands: Does your leadership make your wife's submission a pleasure or a problem?

> *TIP:* *Be prepared to offer your own experience at this point.*

HOMEBUILDERS PRINCIPLE #6:

Submission is a woman's spiritual *response* that encourages her husband to fulfill his spiritual role. Submission is essential to the man's success as a servant-leader.

> *TIP:* *Emphasize that submission is not the wife's role—it is her response to her husband's role. He needs her to willingly submit in order for him to fulfill his responsibility as servant-leader. If she contends or fights with him for control, then it will be very difficult for him to serve and lead her. (Note: The wife's core role will be examined in the next session.)*

B. Stumbling Blocks to Submission

Notice in Ephesians 5:22 (and elsewhere) that husbands are never told to make their wives submit. The appeal to submit in verse 22 is ultimately an issue between a woman and her Lord. Nevertheless, it is an issue with numerous stumbling blocks and tough questions! For instance:

1. What if my husband is not a Christian? How does 1 Peter 3:1,2 encourage a wife in this situation?

2. How do I respond to my husband's inconsistencies and failures as a servant-leader? (Colossians 3:12,13 and Galatians 6:1 would be helpful starting places in answering such a question.)

3. What if my husband wants me to do something wrong or illegal? How does the clarifying attached to the command "be subject to your husbands" in Colossians 3:18 help in answering this? (See also the following Word of Caution #1.)

4. What if I am at times mistreated? What advice does 1 Peter 3:9-12 offer?

> ***TIP:*** *Call on a husband to read aloud the paragraph beginning "Notice in Ephesians 5:22 (and elsewhere)...." Assign each couple one of the tough questions. Instruct them to look up the Scripture reference which accompanies their question, then prepare an answer to share with the group. After a few minutes, call on each couple to respond to their question. Be aware that any of these questions pose enough problems to warrant a lengthy discussion. It will be best to provide fairly brief answers and suggest that couples who actually face any of these situations should spend additional time dealing with the issue—and perhaps seeking competent Christian guidance.*

> **NOTE:** *In any extreme case of mistreatment (i.e., physical abuse, destructive addictions, ongoing adultery, etc.), help should be sought immediately. James Dobson's book* Love Must Be Tough[2] *offers helpful insight for women in such situations.*

5. Isn't submission demeaning to women? Is it demeaning in 1 Corinthians 11:3 and Ephesians 5:21? (See Word of Caution #2.)

WORD OF CAUTION #1: The principle of submission never includes being asked to disobey other scriptural principles. A man's leadership over his wife is meant to fulfill the Scripture in their marriage, not violate it (John 14:15).

WORD OF CAUTION #2: In the name of equality, some women have sought to challenge or share the leadership role given to their husbands. A man who properly understands his role biblically will struggle enough with what that role requires of him. If challenged or competed with, many men quickly give up and excuse themselves from their responsibilities. In homes where women seek to lead, men leave...often they withdraw in psychological, emotional and spiritual ways.

> **TIP:** *Conclude the discussion with a brief comment, "Just as servant-leadership is a very difficult thing for a man to practice, so submission is hard for a woman in today's world. However, rather than ignoring or discounting this biblical role and response, we must continue to study, pray and talk together to support one another in fulfilling the high calling of God in our marriages."*

---

2. (Waco, TX: Word Books, 1983.)

V. SUMMARY *(1 minute)*

This session has sought to define accurately the role conferred upon a man by God in marriage. It is a position of leadership unique by any human standard, primarily because it is so lacking in the "me first" mentality! Husbands who serve their wife and children, who seek their family's best interest, who give direction along biblical lines—these men are the servant-leaders who lead as they were intended to. They will rarely lack followers.

Construction

(to be completed as a couple)
(5-10 minutes)

*This **Construction** will help couples communicate their thoughts and feelings about the husband's role as servant-leader and the wife's response of submission. Instruct couples to take several minutes individually to write their responses to the study guide instructions before sharing their conclusions.*

State when you will call time for them to end their discussion and pray together before regathering as a group.

1. Wives, write down one illustration from your marriage where your husband has exemplified the servant-leader role as discussed in this session.

2. Husbands, write down how you feel about the role responsibilities set forth in this session. What one adjustment could you make right now that would help in fulfilling the leadership call God has on your life?

3. Share your conclusions with one another.

Make a Date

> Make a date with your mate to meet in the next few days to complete **HomeBuilders Project #4**.
>
> Date   Time   Location

*Encourage couples not to slack off on spending time together each week. Instruct them to take out their calendars and write down the time they will meet this week to complete **Home-Builders Project #4**.*

Briefly preview this week's project, calling attention to the Individual and Interaction sections. Stress the importance of ending the project with a specific plan of action. Also, the prayer time which concludes the interaction is of great value.

Recommended Reading

Improving Your Serve, by Charles Swindoll.

This book offers accurate, clear and practical help from the Scriptures on how to develop a servant's heart. The key is a willing heart.

Straight Talk to Men and Their Wives, by James Dobson.

This book is for every husband who wants to know what it means to be a man: how he should relate to his wife, his children, his work and his God.

Dismiss with prayer and a time of fellowship.

HOMEBUILDERS PROJECT #4

Individually: 10-15 minutes

1. Review this session in its entirety.

2. Concentrate specifically on the three leadership responsibilities for servant-leaders (Section III), reviewing and recalling the comments made by the group.

Interact as a Couple: 30-40 minutes

1. Discuss together these three areas of responsibility, then agree upon one that, at present, you both feel needs attention and further refinement.

2. Answer specifically the following questions:

a. Husband: What practical steps can you now take as a result of this discussion with your wife which would demonstrate to her the role of a servant-leader?

b. Wife: What helpful expression of submissiveness could you offer to your husband's effort that would both affirm and encourage him in his leadership role?

3. Commit to a plan of action.

4. Conclude with a time of prayer together. You might specifically...

a. Thank God for outlining in His Word how a marriage is to work (Proverbs 16:20).

b. Confess your failures in your marriage, knowing that He is always ready to forgive (1 John 1:9).

c. Ask His help so that you might succeed in the plan of action just determined (Proverbs 16:3,9).

d. Praise Him that He will never leave you nor forsake you (Hebrews 13:5).

Remember to bring your calendar for **Make a Date** to the next session.

ROLE RESPONSIBILITIES FOR THE WOMAN

OBJECTIVES

You will help your group accurately define the wife's core role in marriage as you lead the group to:

- Examine scriptural instructions about a woman's role in marriage;

- Consider how a woman can apply her scriptural responsibilities in today's society;

- Identify the appropriate response by which the husband can support his wife in fulfilling her role; and

- Discuss specific actions to bring improvement in fulfilling the biblical roles within marriage.

OVERALL COMMENTS

In this session, as in all others, keep attention focused on the big idea. In this case it is accurately understanding the woman's core role in marriage: helper-homemaker. Just as some of the men may have struggled to accept their role as servant-leader, some women will come to the terms "helper" and "homemaker" with built-in resistance. Your acceptance of them and their struggles is vital to help them remain open to the biblical pattern.

Focus

A woman's role in marriage,
though different from a man's,
is equally important. For her, the
divine challenge is that of being a
helper-homemaker.

Warm Up

(5-10 minutes)

1. There is much controversy today concerning a woman's role. If you could see the contemporary family acted out on a stage, would the woman's role be that of:

_____ The Heroine   _____ The Martyr

_____ The Victim   _____ The Extra

_____ The Villain   _____

2. Check one and tell why.

> *TIP: Invite the women to share their response to the **Warm Up** questions. After each one has had a chance to comment, ask if the men have any different thoughts about the woman's role in the drama of contemporary family life. Be sure to lead people to tell why they made the selection they did.*

(45-60 minutes)

I. GOD'S CORE ROLE FOR WIVES
(15-20 minutes)

A. Define a core role.

> **ANSWER:** *The central responsibility which a husband or wife fulfills to build the structure of a marriage.*

B. What distinctives were made between core roles and comprehensive life-styles in Session Four?

> **TIP:** *You may want to read aloud the "Very Important Announcement" from Session Four. Emphasize that the topic of today's session is what woman's core concern should be, recognizing that there are many other things a woman can, will, and should be doing throughout her life.*

Call on one of the husbands to read aloud.

HOMEBUILDERS PRINCIPLE #7:
It is crucial that a wife's role as helper and homemaker be accurately defined before it can be accurately fulfilled.

II. DEFINING THE ROLE OF HELPER-HOMEMAKER *(15-20 minutes)*

A. The Wife as "Helper"

"Then the Lord God said, 'It is not good for the man to be alone; I will make him a helper suitable for him'" (Genesis 2:18).

1. Helper: Negatives and Positives

   a. What words immediately come to mind when you think of a woman as a man's "helper"?

   > **ANSWER:** *Typical responses are words such as "assistant," "secretary," "go-fer," "flunky," "servant"—maybe even "slave."*

   b. Do these words have a positive or negative connotation in your mind?

   > **ANSWER:** *Most likely, they will say negative.*

2. Helper: A Title for God

   a. The title of "helper" given to a woman in Genesis 2 is also a title given to God. For example, God is our Helper in Psalm 10:14 and in Isaiah 41:10,13,14. What new perspective does this fact give in understanding a wife's helper role?

   > **ANSWER:** *Instead of viewing woman as the secondary player, this awareness of the meaning of "helper" shows how vital the role is in providing what is lacking in man. Man has gaps in his life—dangerous ones—which woman is uniquely qualified to fill.*

   > **TIP:** *Call on two men to read aloud Psalm 10:14 and Isaiah 41:10,13,14.*

b. What new dignity does it give?

> **TIP:** *Point out that this new perspective on the role of helper gives great dignity to the title.*

3. The Godly Wife

a. Review again how the husband of Proverbs 31 is helped by his wife (according to vv. 10-12). How would verse 12 be demonstrated in practical, everyday ways today?

b. What impact did this woman's assistance have on her husband's public life, according to Proverbs 31:23? In your opinion, how is this success the result of her help? Explain.

4. Husbands: In what ways has your wife been a valued source of help to you? Has it been her trusted counsel? Insight? Work? What? How has she filled up the "gaps" in your life?

Wives: In what areas do you see yourself as especially suited to be your husband's helper?

> **TIP:** *Have individuals work on their lists alone. Invite couples to compare their lists, then have the husbands share one item that was common on both lists. This should be an insightful, positive experience for both husband and wife.*

5. As far as the godly wife is concerned, how is the title "competitor" the opposite of helper?

> **ANSWER:** *The husband needs help to fill the gaps in his life, compensating for his imbalances and blind spots. A helper brings assistance to those weaknesses so that the husband can succeed. A competitor does just the opposite, exploiting those weaknesses for her own advantage and superiority. A competitor also stirs a man to aggression and retaliation—or to withdrawal—rather than to caring and support to meet the woman's needs.*

> **TIP:** *Instruct everyone to read Proverbs 31:23 to find what impact this woman's assistance has on her husband's public life. Invite opinions on how his success is the result of her help.*

6. Secrets of Success

   a. Some wives are better at helping their husbands than other wives. What is their secret of success according to Proverbs 31:30?

   > **ANSWER:** *Fear of the LORD—godliness.*

   b. What is the secret of success found in Proverbs 19:14?[1]

   > **ANSWER:** *Prudence from the Lord—her godliness produces in her growth and maturity, which give her the good judgment or common sense needed in practical matters.*

   > **TIP:** *Comment that, "In other words, wives become*

---

1. "Prudent" in this passage means using good judgment, intelligence, and common sense in practical matters.

*better helpers to meet their husband's needs when they
become better women of God."*

B. The Wife as Homemaker

1. Titus 2:4-5 puts forth a practical list of core role activities for
a wife, part of which addresses her involvement at home.
What are they?

2. Why would the older wives be best suited to encourage the
younger wives in this direction?

> ***ANSWER:*** *Because of their experience and because men
> who say these things may appear to be chauvinistic.*

3. Using the historical footnote on this page, tell why the word
"encourage" in Titus 2:4 is appropriate for this time?[2] What
does all this tell you about women, their pursuits and their
interests in the first century?

> ***ANSWER:*** *Women of the first century were much like
> women today. They were leaving the home with their
> domestic responsibilities to pursue other careers. It
> was against that backdrop that Paul wrote these
> words for older women to encourage younger women*

---

2. The following historical snapshots are enlightening in regard to the women of the first century:
"Emancipation (for women) was as complete then as now....Women worked in shops, or
factories, especially in the textile trades; some became lawyers and doctors; some became
politically powerful...the decay of the ancient faith among the upper classes had washed
away the supernatural supports of marriage, fidelity, and parentage; the passage from farm to
city had made children less of an asset, more of a liability, and a toy; woman wished to be sex-
ually beautiful rather than maternally beautiful." Will Durant, *The Story of Civilization: Cae-
sar and Christ, Vol. III* (New York: Simon & Schuster, 1944), pp. 222, 370.

Before the New Testament age, in the old Roman Republic, "a woman took pride in her fer-
tility." Now, in the time of Jesus and Paul, "she fears it." Jerome Carcopino, *Daily Life in
Ancient Rome* (New Haven: Yale University Press, 1966), p. 93.

to focus their energies on their families. This under-standing may be of vital importance to some in your group who have been led to believe that first-century women were totally relegated to the home, had little or no experience in the wider culture and were totally dominated by men. The truth was exactly the opposite.

TIP: Call on one of the women to read aloud the historical footnote.

4. Encouragement for the Homemaker

a. Wives: Are you being encouraged to give time and attention to your home and family?

b. Who or what are the sources of encouragement?

c. Who or what are the sources of your discouragement?

5. The Homemaker's Impact

a. "That the word of God may not be dishonored" (Titus 2:5). How does this phrase indicate that Paul's emphasis on being at home and with family is more than a mere cultural one, relevant only to the women of the first century?

ANSWER: God's Word is dishonored by Christians who involve themselves in life's pursuits to the detriment of maintaining a godly home. Since God's Word does not pass out of fashion, an issue as central as bringing honor or dishonor on His Word is an issue that transcends cultural fads and trends.

b. How does Isaiah 40:8 further support Paul's statement?

TIP: Read aloud Isaiah 40:8 to further emphasize the permanence of God's Word and its relevance for our lives.

6. The Godly Wife

   a. Let's go back to the "exalted wife" of Proverbs 31. What statement is given about her regarding her home in v. 27?

   ANSWER: *Looks well to the ways of her household.*

   b. Notice the phrase "looks well." It implies attention, creativity and care. Wives: How much time does it take for you to look after your home and children in an attractive, creative and careful way?

   Husbands: How much time do you think it takes?

   TIP: Encourage couples to look at each other's numbers to see how well they communicate with each other about the necessary tasks.

7. What kind of response does this quality homemaker draw out of both husband and children according to Proverbs 31:28-29?

   TIP: Call on a husband to read aloud Proverbs 31:28,29.

III. PERSPECTIVES FOR HUSBANDS
(10-15 minutes)

This session has focused on the role of a woman as helper-homemaker. But what are the implications associated with this role for the husband? What response is required of him as she seeks to fulfill the charge God has given to her?

A. Circle the key words in the verses printed below which describe the kind of response a wife needs from her husband.

"Render to all what is due them...honor to whom honor [is due]" (Romans 13:7).

"Her husband...praises her, saying: 'Many daughters have done nobly, but you excel them all'" (Proverbs 31:28).

"And grant her honor as a fellow heir of the grace of life" (1 Peter 3:7).

> ***ANSWER:*** *Honor and praise are the key concepts to bring out.*

B. Husbands: How are such responses crucial to your wife's success in pursuing her biblical role? Why are they especially important in today's world?

C. Wives: Share with the men some practical ways they could meaningfully encourage you in your role. Tell them why you need this, how often, and how valuable it is to your daily perspective. Husbands: Take notes!

HOMEBUILDERS PRINCIPLE #8:

Honor and praise are the masculine counterparts to submission. They are essential to the wife's success as a helper-homemaker.

TIP: *This principle will provide a revolutionary insight for some men and women in your group. Comment that just as the wife's submission enables the husband to fulfill his role as servant-leader, so the husband's honor and praise enable the wife to fulfill her calling as helper-homemaker. The core roles can only be adequately fulfilled when the mate responds properly.*

While we often hear exhortations for wives to submit, we rarely hear about the masculine counterpart to submission—honor and praise. Any man who is serious about his wife fulfilling her role will make honor and praise priority ingredients in his response to her efforts. Without these she will feel that her role and tasks are inferior and secondary and will do what so many women in our society have done—go looking for something else that will make her feel good about herself.

IV. SUMMARY *(1 minute)*

How a woman views her husband and her home is not only a statement of her values but also the source of her values. It is clear from Scripture that a wife plays a unique role in her husband's success as a man. He needs a helper, and without his wife's special attention, he is prone to imbalance and blind spots. It is equally clear that God intended for the home and those within it to be a woman's core concern. Though a husband is called to provide for and manage a home, it is the wife's special calling to *make* it a home. These divine challenges are at the heart of her calling as a wife.

> ***TIP:*** *Call on one of the wives to read aloud the summary statement.*

Construction

(to be completed as a couple)
(5-10 minutes)

This project provides two alternatives. The first involves a general review of the points dealt with in this session. The second addresses issues faced when the wife works outside the home and tries to balance her core calling with the demands of another career.

*Instruct couples to look over the two projects and decide which one they prefer to do. Explain when you will call time so they can pray together before regathering as a group. If there is not time for them to finish the project, they can do so at the start of their **HomeBuilders Project** during the week. Allow them to move where they can meet with some privacy.*

This **Construction** time offers you a choice of two alternatives. The first project is more general in nature, overviewing this session as a whole. The second project is much more specific. It focuses on the struggle some wives who work outside the home have in balancing their career with their core calling. As a couple, choose the project that best applies to your situation. If you need more time than the **Construction** sequence allows, start off your **HomeBuilders Project** by finishing up any incomplete discussion.

PROJECT ALTERNATIVE ONE

1. Husbands: Write down one illustration from your marriage where your wife has exemplified the helper-homemaker role discussed in this session.

In what specific area are you presently in need of her help?

2. Wives: Write down how you feel about the core role responsibilities set forth in this session. What one adjustment could you make right now that would help in fulfilling this domestic call God has on your life?

3. Share your conclusions with one another.

PROJECT ALTERNATIVE TWO

1. As already stated, this project addresses women who work outside the home. The Scriptures, of course, do not expressly prohibit a woman from having a career. In fact, very little is said on this issue. Instead, the Scriptures focus on the priorities, values and roles that insure success for one's marriage and family. For a wife, the emphasis is on the support of her husband, the priority of her children and the management of the home. Therefore, these should become the fundamental considerations when addressing work outside the home. They will, as any woman knows, raise serious questions about work that must be squarely faced. Wives: With the help and interaction of your husbands, answer the following questions.

a. Am I attempting to meet my needs and fulfill my life primarily through a career rather than through my relationship with God, His word and the dynamics of my family?

b. Will my husband and children (if any) receive the love and attention they need to succeed?

c. Is there a real need for me to work or is the motivation one of material or personal wants?

d. Does my work away from home hinder my ability in fulfilling my core role?

e. Does my husband agree with my desire for a career outside of the home? (A lack of oneness here can be critical.)

f. If applicable, would he be supportive of my desire to return home on a full-time basis?

2. Titus 2:5 exhorts a wife to be "sensible" regarding her life. Clearly, there are "seasons" in a marriage when a vocation outside the home for a woman is more appropriate and sensible than at other times. Consider the following illustration.

A Marriage Life Cycle for Couples with Children

a. As a couple, evaluate in which seasons work outside the home would best complement God's role call on a wife. In which seasons would outside work tend to conflict most with God's call? How do these observations apply to your present situation?

SEASON 1: Married but without children	SEASON 2: Preschoolers	SEASON 3: Grade Schoolers thru High School	SEASON 4: College Age: Some Children Still at Home	SEASON 5: The Empty Nest

b. What reminder does Proverbs 14:1 give as a woman addresses these questions and considerations of work and family?

c. What, if any, action steps do you need to take as a result of this discussion?

Make a Date

*Encourage couples not to slack off on spending time together each week. Instruct them to use their calendars to select the time they will meet this week to complete **HomeBuilders Project #5**.*

Make a date with your mate to meet in the next few days to complete **HomeBuilders Project #5**.

| Date | Time | Location |

Recommended Reading

A Mother's Heart, by Jean Fleming.

This book tells how you can take a spiritual inventory of your child, how to thoughtfully pray for him, creatively love him and teach him about who God is and what He teaches about life.

Dismiss with prayer and a time of fellowship.

HOMEBUILDERS PROJECT #5

Individually: 10-15 minutes

1. Review this session in its entirety. Concentrate specifically on the helper and homemaker aspects of the wife's role.

2. Husbands: How often do you praise your wife for the special role she plays in your life and the lives of your children?

Record in the space below how and how often you have honored her for specifically being a helper, mother and homemaker.

Wives: Try to remember times when your husband has so honored you.

Interact as a Couple: 30-40 minutes

1. Which of the two aspects of a wife's role do you both feel at present needs attention and further refinement?

2. Answer the following questions:

a. Wives: What practical steps can you define that would address the area of concern identified in Question 1?

b. Husbands: What word of praise or act of honor could you attach to your wife's effort that would affirm, motivate and encourage her in her helper-homemaker role?

3. Conclude with a time of prayer together.

Remember to bring your calendar for **Make a Date**
to the next session.

SUCCEEDING IN THE SPIRIT

OBJECTIVES

You will help your group members discover the Holy Spirit's role in their marital success as you guide them to:

- Examine Scripture dealing with the Holy Spirit's equipping for effective living;
- Identify factors which interfere with the Holy Spirit's help for their marriages;
- Discuss ways of overcoming interference with the Holy Spirit; and
- Discover how God's power can become effective in their marriages.

OVERALL COMMENTS

1. This session emphasizes the role of the Holy Spirit in helping a couple appreciate their differences, honor one another and fulfill their roles. There must be a supernatural Helper for marriages to succeed.
2. The key aspect to be emphasized throughout the session is the will—making the right choice when the Holy Spirit whispers God's Word in your heart. Your own experience—struggles and victories—in yielding your life and marriage to the Spirit will help take this session from the realm of the theoretical to a level of meaningful application.

Focus

Every man and woman has a natural resistance to resolving their gender differences and fulfilling the roles and responsibilities set forth in Scripture for their marriage. Therefore, a supernatural effort is required for God's calling on a marriage to be realized.

Warm Up

(10-15 minutes)

1. Below is a succinct summary of this HomeBuilders study so far. As you review it, what specific insights, key Scriptures and principles from the past five sessions does the outline bring to mind? Record these recollections in the space at the top of the next page.

Issues	Husband	Wife
Resolving Gender Differences	Understands the Feminine Viewpoint	Understands the Masculine Viewpoint
Special Needs	Respect	Love
Core-Role Responsibility	Servant-Leader	Helper-Homemaker
Response Needed from Mate That Encourages Role Fulfillment	Submission	Honor and Praise
Results Promised:	**Oneness in Marriage**	**Oneness in Marriage**

2. Share your insights with the group.

3. Conclude your **Warm Up** time by focusing on the items listed under "issues" in the previous diagram. If someone were available to help you significantly improve one of these issues (resolving gender differences, role responsibility, etc.) which one would you choose to improve? Indicate your selection by marking it with an *X*.

> **TIP:** *Share your own response first to help people feel safe in being open and honest at this point. After the sharing is completed, point out that in this session they will discover that we do have a Helper—one who is willing and able to come to our aid to help us succeed in those issues we've marked.*

(35-45 minutes)

I. GOD HAS GIVEN US A SUPERNATURAL "HELPER" TO HELP US SUCCEED IN MARRIAGE
(10-15 minutes)

A. In the previous sessions, we have been exploring God's blueprints for marriage. God, however, is not content to just give us these much-needed directions. He also offers His personal assistance in getting the job done.

1. What promise does Jesus make to His followers in John 14:16-18?

> *ANSWER:* *God would send His Helper to be with them forever.*

2. What is another name for this Helper in verse 17?

> *ANSWER:* *The Spirit of truth.*

In verse 26?

> *ANSWER:* *The Holy Spirit.*

3. The help Jesus promised that the Spirit would give to the disciples for their lives is the same help the Spirit offers to us for our marriages. What is this very special assistance as stated in verse 26?

> *ANSWER:* *"He will teach you all things, and bring to your remembrance all that I said to you." The disciples had listened to Jesus' words for several years. Now these words would be recalled to their memory in specific situations by the Holy Spirit. The Spirit does the same for us with the Word we have studied, reminding us at just the right moment of the understandings we have gained about God's intentions for our marriage.*
>
> *NOTE:* *This is the most important question of the session, for the help Jesus promised the Spirit would give to the disciples for their lives is the same help the Spirit offers to us for our marriages.*

B. How would you see this kind of help being manifested and experienced in your marriage? How would it make a difference? Can you give a personal example?

> **TIP:** *Share an experience of your own in which you have had the Holy Spirit bring to your awareness a specific thing God's Word says about marriage. Tell how yielding to that principle allowed the Holy Spirit's power to be released in that situation.*
>
> *Be sure that the responses to Question 3 reveal that the Holy Spirit brings to remembrance and helps us understand the Word of God, enabling us to discern what to do in a given situation. He nudges us secretly in our hearts and minds with a small but authoritative voice. Most Christians have had times in their lives when, in the midst of a situation, God has brought to mind a truth from Scripture, illuminating the action they should take. Emphasize the Holy Spirit's role as a Counselor, always going with us, reminding us of what we need to remember to help us do what we need to do.*

HOMEBUILDERS PRINCIPLE #9:

The Holy Spirit will be faithful to remind us of God's Word if we are faithful in learning it.

II. WHAT HINDERS THE HELPER
(15-20 minutes)

A. Within every man and woman there is an evil impulse that rejects God's directions and resists God's help. This streak of independence (Isaiah 53:6) found its way into the heart of humanity when Adam and Eve first disobeyed God (Romans

5:12). It has been passed along to all subsequent generations.

1. Resistance to God's plan

   a. How does Romans 8:5-8 express this natural resistance?

> ***ANSWER:*** *Those who walk by the flesh set their minds on things of the flesh (things and values of this natural world), not on the Word of God. The ways of the world promote selfish attitudes and actions, rather than the selfless attitudes of servant and helper which Scripture shows are the responses which build solid marriages.*

   b. What label does Paul use here to describe this resistance?

> ***ANSWER:*** *Death, hostility.*

How the Flesh Manifests Itself in a Marriage

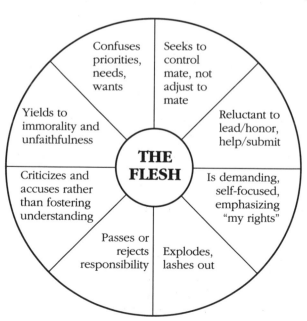

- Confuses priorities, needs, wants
- Seeks to control mate, not adjust to mate
- Yields to immorality and unfaithfulness
- Reluctant to lead/honor, help/submit
- **THE FLESH**
- Criticizes and accuses rather than fostering understanding
- Is demanding, self-focused, emphasizing "my rights"
- Passes or rejects responsibility
- Explodes, lashes out

2. How is "the flesh" further described in Galatians 5:19-21?

> ***ANSWER:*** *A life-style of immorality, impurity, idolatry, anger, disputes, factions, etc.*

3. The power of this resistance

   a. Using Romans 7:18-21 as a reference point, describe how the flesh influences those seeking to construct their marriage according to God's blueprints.

   > ***ANSWER:*** *While many people desire a godly, strong marriage, their minds are focused on the flesh—on this world—so that they are not able to achieve the results they want. The dominance of their mind-set prevents them from moving beyond the wish for a better marriage, and they continually fail at their good intentions.*

   b. In what ways have you experienced the fruit of the flesh limiting the success of your marriage? (Resist pointing fingers; personalize.)

   > ***TIP:*** *Be prepared to share your own unsuccessful efforts to build a good marriage with a mind set on this world. Caution people to talk only about their own shortcomings, not about their mate's.*

HOMEBUILDERS PRINCIPLE #10:

The fuel that most often energizes the flesh is our world
(1 John 2:15,16; Jude 19).

> *TIP: Call on someone to read 1 John 2:15-16 and Jude 19. Emphasize the word "fuel" in the **Home-Builders Principle**. When we take in worldly counsel, focus on worldly things and develop our marriages around what we see in the movies or what others tell us, we are energizing our flesh to move us to live for ourselves. The flesh grows stronger and stronger as we feed our minds and our desires on the temporal rather than eternal. The flesh is stimulated by the messages of the world. The next segment of the session provides the solution to how we can arrest this process and increase the Holy Spirit's effectiveness in our lives.*

B. Overcoming the Flesh

1. God has placed His Holy Spirit within every Christian so that the power of the flesh can be opposed and overcome. Having two opposing forces within us creates an ongoing internal conflict which most of us feel every day. Notice how this conflict is expressed in Galatians 5:16-17.

> *ANSWER: They are in opposition to one another.*

> *TIP: Point out that every Christian has the freedom of choice to yield to either the flesh or the Holy Spirit. Our free choice is the determining factor; a conscious act of the will is always involved. No one accidentally slides into obedience to the Spirit or into allegiance to the flesh. Call on a group member to read aloud Galatians 5:16-17 and tell how these verses describe the status of the flesh and the Spirit within us.*

Therefore, in the heart of every Christian is the same struggle:

2. The daily ongoing skirmishes that take place between the flesh and God's Spirit do not in themselves determine the outcome. In other words, who wins in your heart and ultimately in your life is not determined by those forces alone. *Who wins is determined by you...by an act of your will!* It is your choice that unleashes either the power of the flesh or the power of the Spirit to influence and rule in that moment of your life...and then in the next moment...and the next.

   a. How does Paul make it clear that our choice is the determining factor...

   In Romans 6:12,13?

   In Romans 8:12,13?

   ANSWER: *We must present (give) ourselves to God; we must put to death the deeds of the body.*

   TIP: *Divide your group in half; assign one group to look up Romans 6:12,13 while the rest look at Romans*

8:12,13. Instruct them to find how Paul defines our choice as the determining factor in whether the flesh or the Spirit is in control. Allow time for people to read and think, then invite volunteers from each group to tell what they discovered.

b. How does Moses say it in Deuteronomy 30:19?

ANSWER: *Choose life.*

TIP: *Summarize the main point of the verses that have just been read: "As we study God's Word and come to understand His will and His ways, we can depend on the Holy Spirit to bring to the surface the principles that apply to the situation we face, showing us the direction we should follow. At that moment, we must present ourselves to God, we must put to death the temptation of the flesh and we must choose to obey what the Holy Spirit has brought to our attention."*

How the Holy Spirit Manifests Himself in a Marriage

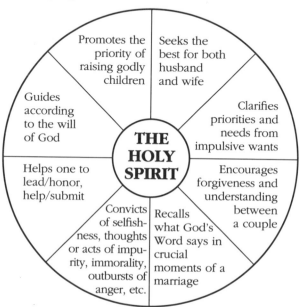

3. If we choose to yield ourselves to the influence of God's Spirit, what will be the powerful results? See Galatians 5:22,23.

ANSWER: Love, joy, peace, etc.

When we submit to God's Spirit, good things happen!

HOMEBUILDERS PRINCIPLE #11:

The Holy Spirit helps fulfill in us what God requires of us in marriage.

IMPORTANT NOTE!
If you sense that anyone in your group is not a Christian, this might be a good time to take a few moments to explain the gospel. Refer to "The Four Spiritual Laws" section at the end of the leader's guides and study guides.

We suggest that you explain briefly how you can become a Christian and the differences that walking with Christ has made in your life. Then read through The Four Spiritual Laws presentation.

Also included at the end of the leader's guides and study guides is a longer explanation of the Holy Spirit and His power in our lives. Suggest to your group members that they read through this on their own.

4. Describe one instance in your own marriage where you believe you have yielded to God's Spirit and experienced the fruit and power He promised.

HOMEBUILDERS PRINCIPLE #12:

The fuel that most often energizes the Spirit is God's Word
(2 Timothy 3:16,17; Colossians 3:16a).

TIP: *Ask two others to read aloud 2 Timothy 3:16,17 and Colossians 3:16a. Point out the contrast with* ***HomeBuilders Principle #10****, which talks about the fuel that energizes the flesh. The Word of God is the key in fueling the Spirit of God's recollections in the day-to-day experiences of marriage. When the Spirit reminds us of truth, we choose to either yield or disobey. The great benefits seen are the results of yielding ourselves to the influence of God's Spirit.*

III. RELEASING GOD'S POWER IN YOUR MARRIAGE *(10-15 minutes)*

A. Releasing God's power in your marriage depends on several factors:

1. It depends on whom I believe is right—God's Word or the flesh.

2. It depends on whose voice I listen to—the voice of the Spirit or the voice of my flesh.

3. It depends on whom I love the most—God or the flesh.

4. Finally and most important, it depends in the end on whom I yield and submit to—God's Spirit or the flesh.

> *TIP:* *Read aloud each of the four factors listed in the study guide while group members follow along silently. Pause after each of the statements and instruct*

*people to privately circle whom they really do believe,
listen to, love and yield to. Explain that this exercise
helps them to personalize why God's power is or is not
being effective in their marriage.*

B. This form of submission is for every Christian husband and
wife! It is a submission that crowns a marriage with God's
blessing. When a man and woman submit to the Holy Spirit—who is seeking to apply God's Word to a marriage—then
God's power is released. This submission is not to be
thought of as a one-time event, but a moment-by-moment
walk with God and struggle against the flesh.

HOMEBUILDERS PRINCIPLE #13:

A husband and wife can resolve gender differences, respond to unique needs and fulfill respective roles only as they submit by faith to God's Spirit and live under His special influence (Ephesians 5:18).

TIP: *Read aloud Ephesians 5:18. Summarize this study, "Gaining the benefit of the supernatural Helper in our marriage fol-
lows this sequence of events."*
1. *We must first learn God's Word. When we do so, we hide God's
Word in our mind and it transforms our thinking.*
2. *In the day-to-day of marriage, God's Spirit brings up God's
Word and applies it to the specific situations we face.*
3. *At this point, we can either yield to what the Spirit is nudging
us to do—or we can disobey.*
4. *If we yield, then and only then is the power of God's Spirit
released in our marriage and the fruit of His Spirit grows in
our relationship. The power and the fruit come after we yield,
not before.*

Construction

(to be completed as a couple)
(5-10 minutes)

*This **Construction** section leads a couple to examine specific areas in their marriage in which they desire the Holy Spirit to help them.*

*SPECIAL NOTE: Before having the couples respond to these questions, point out that if the husband and wife are at significantly different levels in their desire to yield to the Holy Spirit in their marriage, the **Construction** and **Home-Builders Project** will be very difficult. The easiest thing would be to avoid the issue and just let each person's spiritual position be a totally private matter. However, it is unfortunate when a husband and wife block each other from their spiritual lives, for then they rob each other of the awareness of the Spirit's working within them both for their mutual growth and benefit.*

*Encourage couples to focus in the **Construction** on areas of agreement and not to be detoured into areas in which they might not see eye-to-eye. By building on mutually shared commitments first, they strengthen themselves to deal with more difficult areas later on.*

Recommend that, if the concept of walking in the Spirit is a new concept to anyone, the couple should plan to take time this week to read the materials listed under recommended reading—especially The Holy Spirit, *by Bill Bright. Most people do not understand the Spirit-filled life simply because they have not studied it.*

Instruct the couples to find a place where they can talk together comfortably and privately. Explain how much time the couples will have for meeting together and when you will give the signal for them to conclude their time in prayer before regathering as a group.

1. What new understanding of your marriage do you now have as a result of this session on the Holy Spirit?

2. What one area in your lives needs the powerful influence of the Holy Spirit right now?

3. In light of the session, how would you expect the Holy Spirit to give you realistic help in this area? How would He make a difference?

4. What could you do to help the Holy Spirit help you?

Make a Date

Make a date with your mate to meet in the next few days to complete **HomeBuilders Project #6**.

_____ _____ _____
Date   Time   Location

*Instruct couples to take out their calendars and set a time to meet together to complete **HomeBuilders Project #6**. Point out that this project touches on very deep, probably sensitive areas in everyone's life. Take time to walk the couples through the project, helping them understand what they are to do, preparing them for some significant personal probing and encouraging them to be supportive and accepting of each other, even if there are differences in their levels of commitment to the issues raised in this session.*

Suggest some possible action steps people might decide on at the conclusion. For example, a person who does not know much Scripture might write down, "I'm going to get into a Bible study to learn the Scriptures, especially what they say about marriage." Or perhaps, "I'm going to read up on the Holy Spirit." Or, "I'm going to focus on an area where I'm struggling and begin to saturate myself with insight from God's Word in that area." Point out that they will finish the project by meeting together again to share the commitments they have made.

Recommended Reading

The Holy Spirit, by Bill Bright.

In this book, Bill Bright helps you discover the secret of living beyond normal human limits by tapping into the power of God through the Holy Spirit.

Transferable Concepts for Powerful Living, by Bill Bright.

1. *How to Be Sure You Are a Christian*
2. *How to Experience God's Love and Forgiveness*
3. *How to Be Filled with the Spirit*
4. *How to Walk in the Spirit*

These booklets explain the "how-to's" of consistent, successful Christian living.

> **TIP:** *Express your own availability to meet individually with anyone to talk about the Holy Spirit in his or her life and marriage.*

Dismiss in prayer, followed by an informal time of fellowship and refreshments.

HomeBuilders Project #6

Interact as a Couple: 25-30 minutes

1. Review: Share with each other two or three things that really spoke to you from Session Six.

2. What most hinders your walk with the Holy Spirit and keeps you from yielding to His inward promptings? Check one of the choices below, then discuss together.

☐ Pride
☐ Unbelief (Hebrews 11:6)
☐ Being weak to respond to His promptings
☐ Fear (John 10:10)
☐ Ignorance of the Scripture and apparent inability to recognize the "voice" of the Spirit when He speaks (Hebrews 5:13,14)
☐ Unrepentant sin/guilt (1 John 1:9)
☐ Being in love with the things in the world
☐ My marriage
☐ Ignorance of the Holy Spirit and His ministry
☐ Peer pressure
☐ Other

Individually: 15 minutes

1. Silently read Galatians 5:25.

2. Ask yourself the following questions:

Am I willing to give the Holy Spirit complete control of my life in all areas?

☐ Yes   ☐ No

Am I willing to address aggressively that area which I just indicated most hinders my walk with the Holy Spirit?

☐ Yes   ☐ No

3. If your answer was yes to the questions above, write below the specific steps you intend to take to address that area and when you intend to take each one.

<u>Step</u>   <u>Date</u>

4. Conclude in prayer by telling God what you want to do. Ask for His help in accomplishing your plan. Tell Him you want to know how to walk daily with the Holy Spirit so that your marriage and all of your life will be enriched. Ask God to make you sensitive to the Holy Spirit's personal leading. Say to Him that you are willing for Him to control your life. Commit to God that you will submit to the Holy Spirit when He does so lead. Thank Him by faith that He will answer your prayers.

Interact as a Couple: 5-10 minutes

1. Come back together and share your commitments with one another.

Remember to bring your calendar for **Make a Date**
to the next session.

GIFTS FOR ANOTHER GENERATION

OBJECTIVES

You will help your group members to instill positive gender identification in their children as you lead them to:

- Evaluate the impact of the gender roles their children have observed at home;
- Examine three "gifts" they can leave their children;
- Discover the biblical promises to those who effectively guide their children; and
- Commit to specific action to deal with stumbling blocks which impede the effective guidance of their children.

OVERALL COMMENTS

1. This session turns the focus of roles, needs and responses toward how they affect the success of our children in the next generation. Stress how important it is for children to have clarity about what it means to be a man or a woman and how to relate to the opposite sex. Positive gender identification is essential in building a healthy self-concept that can face the challenges of life in this world. Sadly, many children leave their homes as emotional, psychological and social cripples because mom and dad did not help them come to know who they are.

2. Be aware of those couples in your group who do not have children or whose children are grown. Those without children can benefit from this session by thinking into the future, when they may have children, or by applying these insights to their responsibility to the children of friends and relatives. Those whose children are grown may be able to add words of wisdom and experience to the discussion. It's also possible that some may feel regret about errors they made in the past and about the lack of opportunity to communicate new insights to children who have left home. Encourage these people to explore ways in which they can continue to build relationships and beneficial communication with their children and grandchildren.

Focus

Marriage is the mold that shapes our children's most basic understanding of themselves. Role and gender confusion in these formative years often has negative consequences in their self-identities for a lifetime. Therefore, a biblical perspective on what it means to be "a man" and what it means to be "a woman," demonstrated through the lives of parents, is critical to our children's success.

(5-10 minutes)

1. How has this series affected your marriage? List below one change you believe has the best chance of being *long-lasting* in your marriage. Tell why.

> **TIP:** *Be prepared to share your own example to help make this an encouraging time in which people can sense they have made real progress.*

2. List below one "gift" ("gifts" being defined as a particular way of life, habit, value, or perspective) that either your mother or father's life has given you which has made your marriage better or your role as a husband or wife easier.

> **TIP:** *Keep the focus of this activity positive. Some individuals may find it hard to think positively here, recalling mostly negatives or lacks which have hurt them in their marriage relationship. It can be helpful for a person to think of some positive qualities they feel they have developed, then look for indications of those qualities in their memories of their parents. There is great value in looking below the surface memories to find helpful perspectives, values, habits, or attitudes which have been forgotten.*

3. What is one "gift" you now wish they would have given you? Why?

TIP: Encourage your group that this sharing will help them see how important it is that they leave strengths in their own children to equip them for the challenges of their marriages.

Blueprints

(35-55 minutes)

I. THE LAW OF LIFE-STYLE *(10-15 minutes)*

A. Identity and Values

1. Before parents can impart to their children a clear sense of identity and direction, they must possess these qualities themselves. This is the law of life-style. Research has demonstrated that self-esteem and self-confidence, two essential features in the makeup of a child's personality, are directly related to parents possessing and communicating a clear idea of what their values are.[1]

   Keeping in mind the statement above, which of the following life-styles would you think most harmful to a child in terms of developing a strong and well-defined sense of self-identity and role? Check one and tell why:

   ☐ Parents who communicate Christian values in their marriage and live them out.

   ☐ Parents who communicate secular values in their marriage and live them out.

   ☐ Parents who communicate Christian values in their marriage and live out secular values.

---

1. W. Peter Blitchington, *Sex Roles and the Christian Family* (Wheaton, IL: Tyndale House Publishers, 1981), p. 107.

TIP: The key phrase in the opening paragraph is "possessing and communicating."

Instruct people to underline this phrase to help them think about the values they possess and communicate to their children.

2. How would you apply the story of Luke 6:46-49 to the kind of home you marked? Be specific.

B. Role and Gender Distinctives

1. Role and gender confusion in the next generation is the result of life-style confusion in today's homes. It is recycled misery. For children to first notice, then understand, and finally honor basic male and female differences and role patterns, parents must make the golden connection between lips and living. That's the law of life-style.

TIP: Call on someone to read aloud the paragraph about role and gender confusion. Point out that the issue is not whether a boy will grow up to be a sissy if he sees his dad change diapers or work in the kitchen. The issue is the need for children to see their parents live out their core roles.

HOMEBUILDERS PRINCIPLE #14:

You will leave in your children what you have lived out in your home.

---

2. "Parents mold and shape the child's developing personality and give him most of the advantages (or disadvantages) that he will enjoy in later years."[2]

What "advantages" from your marriage would you want to leave your children in light of this series of sessions?

> **TIP:** *Instruct each couple to spend a few minutes together dreaming about the advantages they want to leave their children. After a few minutes, invite each couple to tell about one advantage to the rest of the group.*

II. THREE "GIFTS" FOR YOUR CHILDREN'S FUTURE *(25-30 minutes)*

A. Gift #1: An insightful understanding of the differences and similarities between men and women.

1. According to Psalm 119:97-100,104,105, where should parents go for such insights? Recall what you learned in Session One.

> **ANSWER:** *Scripture is central in providing solutions to problems and insightful understanding of the unique natures of men and women.*

> **TIP:** *Call on two group members to read aloud Psalm 119:97-100 and verses 104, 105.*

---

2. W. Peter Blitchington, *Sex Roles and the Christian Family* (Wheaton, IL: Tyndale House Publishers, 1981), p. 18.

2. According to Proverbs 1:8,9, both mom and dad bear responsibility for teaching these vital truths to their children. Of the two, who usually seems to have the greater difficulty in carrying out this responsibility, in your opinion?

> ***ANSWER:*** *While answers will vary depending on the family situations, in most cases the father, the one who usually spends the least time with the children, has the most difficulty teaching these vital truths.*

3. What insight does Psalm 78:5-8 offer in this regard? Who is the intended recipient of this command?

> ***ANSWER:*** *God is telling the fathers, the men of Israel, to teach His Word to their children. However, these men had great difficulty doing that, and are criticized in verse 8 because their generation "did not prepare its heart" rightly before God. Their stubborn rebelliousness resulted in their children's not learning to put their confidence in God.*

4. Compare Psalm 78 with Luke 1:13-17. What is the key to accepting this teaching responsibility?

> ***ANSWER:*** *John the Baptist will "make ready a people prepared for the Lord"—just the opposite of the fathers described in Psalm 78, who did not prepare their hearts. One of the evidences of such a prepared heart is that it turns the hearts of the fathers back to the children. Children suddenly become a priority. Dads begin to assume the responsibility of teaching their children. The key to accepting this teaching responsi-*

bility is that the father's heart is "prepared for the Lord."

TIP: *Read aloud Luke 1:13-17 and point out that this message to Zechariah is announcing the fulfillment of a prophecy in Malachi.*

5. How is this first gift being given or prepared for right now in your home? Please describe.

B. **Gift #2:** Practical how-to's in meeting those special needs men and women have.

1. What special needs of women can you recall from our series? List them in the space below. What Scripture can you list next to each which supports your claim that this is a special feminine need?

Special Feminine Need   Scripture

TIP: *Suggest that people look at their notes for Session Two to help them recall.*

2. Husbands: How would your present life-style demonstrate to your children (current or future) that women do have special needs and that you know how to meet them?

TIP: *Share one or two examples from your own experience, including one that shows you still struggle and need to learn more. This will make it easier for the men to be open and honest in this sensitive area.*

Husbands: Take notes on what the other men share. Learn from each other.

3. What special needs did this series reveal men have? List them below and provide a supporting Scripture if you can.

Special Masculine Need	Scripture

4. Wives: How would your present life-style demonstrate to your children (current or future) that men do have special needs and that you know how to meet them?

Wives: Take action on what the other wives share. Learn from each other.

> *TIP: Emphasize that a man's and woman's present life-style demonstrates daily to their children that they know the special needs of their mates and how to meet them.*

C. Gift #3: A strong and accurate desire to fulfill one's biblical role in a marriage.

1. For a son that means a desire to be a _____.

   For a daughter that means a desire to be a _____.

   > *TIP: Ask for a man to complete the statement about the role a son should be led to desire (servant-leader). Ask a woman to do the same for the statement about a daughter (helper-homemaker).*

2. How would the present role you fill in your marriage, and the attitude with which you do so, create in your son or daughter (current or future) a positive desire for the role God will want them to fill? Explain.

> **TIP:** *Instruct each person to think silently about the question, and after several minutes invite volunteers to share their answers.*

D. Summary

1. When we give these "gifts" to our children, we are launching the homes of the future. They will be homes constructed with sound blueprints, clear job descriptions, practical how-to's and vast potential. How is such a home described in Proverbs 24:3,4?

> **ANSWER:** *When we follow wisdom and understanding (i.e., the insights of Scripture), then those who live within our home gain wisdom and understanding for the future.*

2. Notice these "gifts" extend to bless even our grandchildren in Proverbs 13:20-22b. What other insights does this passage reveal?

> **ANSWER:** *The person who walks with those who are wise will be wise. The child whose parents are wise and full of the Scriptures will be wise. But if parents are foolish—resisting God's wisdom—the child will suffer harm and adversity. And the impact continues on to future generations.*

III. GIFTS THAT RETURN *(10 minutes)*

A. Giving such expensive gifts as the ones we have discussed in this session will not go unrewarded in the kingdom of God. Jesus said, "Give, and it will be given to you" (Luke 6:38). Gifts that are given will mean gifts that return.

> ***TIP:*** *Comment briefly that the time, values, examples and instruction that parents give to their children will become one of their primary joys at the end of their lives.*

B. In the following references you will find a sampling of what some of these "return gifts" actually are. Discuss your answers.

> ***TIP:*** *Assign each couple one of the four Scriptures listed. Ask them to read their verse(s) and answer the accompanying question. Then call on each couple to read their verse(s) aloud and share their answer.*

1. Proverbs 23:24,25—How do godly children affect the emotional health of a mom and dad in their later years?

> ***ANSWER:*** *Children who live righteously will bring rejoicing to father and mother.*

Contrast this experience with the one described in Proverbs 17:25.

> ***ANSWER:*** *Children who do the opposite bring their parents grief.*

2. Proverbs 31:10—How would you like to be known for having raised this daughter in your home?

> ***ANSWER:*** *Imagine the joy and pride in having raised a daughter to become such an excellent, godly wife!*

3. Proverbs 31:27,28a—How would you as a mother enjoy this kind of acclaim?

> ***ANSWER:*** *Imagine the deep satisfaction and sense of gratitude for the blessings of such children!*

4. Third John 2-4—What is John's greatest joy?

> ***ANSWER:*** *Speaking of his children in the Lord, which is our ultimate goal for our physical children, John says his greatest joy is to see them walking in the truth.*

HOMEBUILDERS PRINCIPLE #15:

A wise couple knows what life's most promising investments are.

TIP: *Point out that when a couple reaches their later years, it will not be their possessions or achievements that will be their primary joy; instead, their deepest satisfaction will come from having raised godly children who know how to live.*

IV. SUMMARY *(1 minute)*

Congratulate everyone for having completed this HomeBuilders study. Briefly review the entire series using the summary chart. State each of the issues listed and the appropriate distinction for husband and wife. In referring to the "Results Promised" at the bottom of the chart, emphasize that no other possible results could surpass the benefit of "Oneness in Marriage" and producing "Gifted Children"—and no other structure for a marriage could produce these results.

Issues	Husband	Wife
Resolving Gender Differences	Understands the Feminine Viewpoint	Understands the Masculine Viewpoint
Special Needs	Respect	Love
Core-Role Responsibility	Servant-Leader	Helper-Homemaker
Response Needed from Mate That Encourages Role Fulfillment	Submission	Honor and Praise
Help Needed from God	Holy Spirit	Holy Spirit
Results Promised:	**Oneness in Marriage "Gifted" Children**	**Oneness in Marriage "Gifted" Children**

Construction

(to be completed as a couple)
(5-10 minutes)

*This **Construction** section leads couples to identify specific ways in which they can fulfill their biblical responsibilities to guide their children effectively. Be aware of those who do not have children at home. Review the "Comments" at the beginning of this session for ideas to help these couples benefit from this activity.*

Instruct couples to meet privately to complete the project. Announce the time when they should conclude their interaction and conclude in prayer for one another before rejoining the group for some closing instructions.

1. Proverbs 22:6 is the Bible's basic principle on parenting. What does it say?

What hope does it give?

The word "train" in this passage can also mean "dedicate." It is used of dedicating a home in Deuteronomy 20:5.[3] As parents train their children they are actually dedicating the homes of the next generation.

2. For children to be trained rightly, both mom and dad must assume some specific responsibilities. First, look up in the following Scripture the responsibility which applies to you. Record your findings, then discuss the questions which follow.

Husbands: Ephesians 6:4

Wives: Titus 2:3-5

   a. Are you willing to assume this responsibility God is asking of you? Why or why not?

---

3. Derick Kidner, *Proverbs* (London: Intervarsity Press, 1973), p.147.

b. What are the major stumbling blocks in your minds to fulfilling these parental responsibilities?

c. What changes would you need to begin making right now in order to fulfill these biblical responsibilities?

Make a date with your mate to complete the last **Home-Builders Project** this week.

Date	Time	Location

While this is the final group meeting of this study, encourage couples not to bypass **HomeBuilders Project #7***. The actions planned in this time together will be highly significant in the continuing health and growth of each marriage. Call attention to the instruction to send a note to the leader indicating that the project has been completed. The purpose of this is to maintain a sense of accountability and to give a sense of closure to the study.*

Point out the "Individual" section, during which they are to review this last session and summarize specific insights concerning their marriage and their children. This is followed by "Interaction" time to plan some actions they will take to "gift" their children in the next generation. An example is provided.

Call attention to the suggested future project, which focuses backward to the parents of your group members. This may be of particular benefit to those couples who do not have children or whose children are grown.

Encourage couples to make the weekly date a continuing part of their schedule, setting aside and protecting time to focus on each other and the issues they face as a couple.

Join hands with everyone in the group and conclude with a time of group praise for what God has taught you and for the good experiences ahead in each marriage.

HomeBuilders Project #7

Send a note to your group leader indicating that you have completed the following project.

Individually: 10-15 minutes
Review this last session, summarizing below the major insights that spoke specifically to you and your marriage.

Interact as a Couple: 30 minutes

1. Discuss your summations together. What new insights did you gain?

2. What plan of action can you now commit to as parents (or future parents) as a result of this session? List five specific action steps you plan to take that would "gift" your children in the next generation.

Example: Praise my wife regularly in front of my children. Include them in planning special occasions to honor their mother (which hopefully will "gift" sons for honoring their future wives).

Action Step #1:

Action Step #2:

Action Step #3:

Action Step #4:

Action Step #5:

3. Conclude by reading together Proverbs 16:3. Notice the hope it gives. Use its directions to guide you as you conclude this time in prayer.

SUGGESTED FUTURE PROJECT

We began this session by remembering the "gifts" our parents gave to us that have made our marriages better and easier. Of course they did much more than that—much more. Why not take several hours and remember all the good things your parents have done, as well as all the sacrifices they made during your years at home? Write these down. Then organize them into a *written* tribute and present it to one (or both) at a special occasion (their anniversary, Christmas, or a birthday.) Nothing could be more satisfying to a parent than to be remembered and honored in such a way. It will crown the latter part of their life with deep joy. You may find, as many have, that your project is one of your greatest gifts to your parents—one filled with love, healing and untold blessing.

"Honor your Mother and your Father (which is the first commandment with a promise), that it may be well with you, and that you may live long on the earth." (See Ephesians 6:2,3.)

NOTE: *After the group members finish this last session, please encourage them to fill out the evaluation at the end of the study. They can then send them in individually or you could, as the group leader, collect all evaluations and send them in for the group.*

CONCLUSION

WHERE DO YOU GO FROM HERE?

The biblically structured family has probably never been considered chic. As we learned in this study, it wasn't so in Paul's day, nor is it in ours. Today, a biblically arranged marriage has as many critics as it does skeptics. Even within the Christian community, some have sought to explain it away by using all kinds of fanciful theological arguments. But it will weather these storms just as it has done in generation after generation. God's Word is that clear and certain.

Building your marriage upon these truths may not be popular today, but it will be powerful. Some special glimpses of that power have probably already been felt by you through your investment of study, discussion and application together. If the truth within this couples study has at times shaken your marriage, it has done so only to strengthen it. Hopefully, a sense of strengthening has been your experience. But let's not stop here!

If this HomeBuilders Couples Series study has helped you and your marriage, let's go on. And in going on, why not ask other couples to join you. By personally initiating another Home-Builders study, you will not only add additional mortar to your marriage, you will also be a part of strengthening other marriages as well. As Christians, we are not just trying to improve ourselves—we are trying to reach the world! This is our ultimate objective in The HomeBuilders Couples Series. Will you now help us help others?

WILL YOU JOIN US IN "TOUCHING LIVES...CHANGING FAMILIES"?

The following are some practical ways you can make a difference in families today:

1. Gather a group of couples (four to seven) and lead them through the seven sessions of the HomeBuilders study you have just completed.

2. Commit to participate in other HomeBuilders studies, such as *Building Your Marriage* or *Building Your Mate's Self-Esteem.*

3. Begin weekly family nights—teaching your children about Christ, the Bible and the Christian life.

4. Host an Evangelistic Dinner Party—invite your non-Christian friends to your home and as a couple share your faith in Christ and the forgiveness of His gospel.

5. Share the good news of Jesus Christ with neighborhood children.

6. Show the film, *JESUS,* on video as an evangelistic outreach in your neighborhood. For more information, write to:

> Inspirational Media
> 30012 Ivy Glenn Dr., Suite 200
> Laguna Niguel, CA. 92677

7. If you have attended the FamilyLife Marriage Conference, why not assist your pastor in counseling premarrieds using the material you received?

For more information on any of the above ministry opportunities, contact your local church, or write:

> FamilyLife
> P.O. Box 23840
> Little Rock, AR 72221-3840
> (501)223-8663

ABOUT THE AUTHOR:

Robert Lewis has been a teaching pastor at Fellowship Bible Church in Little Rock, Arkansas since 1980. He is a graduate of the University of Arkansas, Western Conservative Baptist Seminary and Talbot Theological Seminary. He has spoken nationally and internationally with the FamilyLife of Campus Crusade for Christ for over 5 years. He also coauthored the book, *Rocking the Roles*. Robert and his wife, Sherard, have been married for 17 years and have 4 children: Elizabeth, Rebekah, Garrett and Mason.

THE FOUR SPIRITUAL LAWS*

Just as there are physical laws that govern the physical universe, so are there spiritual laws that govern your relationship with God.

> **LAW ONE: God loves you and offers a wonderful plan for your life.**

God's Love

"For God so loved the world, that He gave His only begotten Son, that whoever believes in Him should not perish, but have eternal life" (John 3:16).

God's Plan

(Christ speaking) "I came that they might have life, and might have it abundantly" (that it might be full and meaningful) (John 10:10).

Why is it that most people are not experiencing the abundant life? Because...

> **LAW TWO: Man is sinful and separated from God. Therefore, he cannot know and experience God's love and plan for his life.**

Man Is Sinful

"For all have sinned and fall short of the glory of God" (Romans 3:23).

Man was created to have fellowship with God; but, because of his stubborn self-will, chose to go his own independent way, and fellowship with God was broken. This self-will, characterized by an attitude of active rebellion or passive indifference, is evidence of what the Bible calls sin.

Man Is Separated

"For the wages of sin is death" (spiritual separation from God) (Romans 6:23).

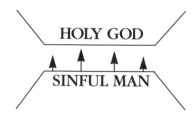

This diagram illustrates that God is holy and man is sinful. A great gulf separates the two. The arrows illustrate that man is continually trying to reach God and the abundant life through his own efforts, such as a good life, philosophy, or religion.

The third law explains the only way to bridge this gulf...

LAW THREE: Jesus Christ is God's only provision for man's sin. Through Him you can know and experience God's love and plan for your life.

He Died in Our Place

"But God demonstrates His own love toward us, in that while we were yet sinners, Christ died for us" (Romans 5:8).

He Rose from the Dead

"Christ died for our sins . . . He was buried . . . He was raised on the third day according to the Scriptures . . . He appeared to [Peter], then to the twelve. After that He appeared to more than five hundred . . ." (1 Corinthians 15:3-6).

He Is the Only Way to God

"Jesus said to him, 'I am the way, and the truth, and the life; no one comes to the Father, but through Me'" (John 14:6).

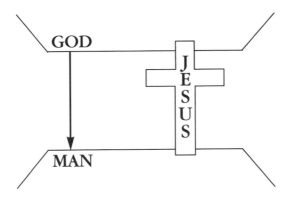

This diagram illustrates that God has bridged the gulf that separates us from Him by sending His Son, Jesus Christ, to die on the cross in our place to pay the penalty for our sins.

It is not enough just to know these three laws . . .

> **LAW FOUR: We must individually receive Jesus Christ as Savior and Lord; then we can know and experience God's love and plan for our lives.**

We Must Receive Christ
"But as many as received Him, to them He gave the right to become children of God, even to those who believe in His name" (John 1:12).

We Receive Christ Through Faith
"For by grace you have been saved through faith; and that not of yourselves, it is the gift of God; not as a result of works, that no one should boast" (Ephesians 2:8,9).

When We Receive Christ, We Experience a New Birth
(Read John 3:1-8.)

We Receive Christ by Personal Invitation
(Christ is speaking) "Behold, I stand at the door and knock; if any one hears My voice and opens the door, I will come in to him" (Revelation 3:20).

Receiving Christ involves turning to God from self (repentance) and trusting Christ to come into our lives to forgive our sins and to make us the kind of people He wants us to be. Just to agree intellectually that Jesus Christ is the Son of God and that He died on the cross for our sins is not enough. Nor is it enough to have an emotional experience. We receive Jesus Christ by faith, as an act of the will.

These two circles represent two kinds of lives:

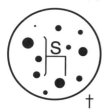

SELF-DIRECTED LIFE

S — Self is on the throne
† — Christ is outside the life
• — Interests are directed by self, often resulting in discord and frustration

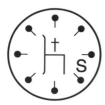

CHRIST-DIRECTED LIFE

† — Christ is in the life and on the throne
S — Self is yielding to Christ
• — Interests are directed by Christ, resulting in harmony with God's plan

Which circle best represents your life?
Which circle would you like to have represent your life?
The following explains how you can receive Christ:

You Can Receive Christ Right Now By Faith Through Prayer

(Prayer is talking with God.)

God knows your heart and is not so concerned with your words as He is with the attitude of your heart. The following is a suggested prayer:

> *Lord Jesus, I need You. Thank You for dying on the cross for my sins. I open the door of my life and receive You as my Savior and Lord. Thank You for forgiving my sins and giving me eternal life. Make me the kind of person You want me to be.*

Does this prayer express the desire of your heart?
If it does, pray this prayer right now, and Christ will come into your life, as He promised.

HAVE YOU MADE THE WONDERFUL DISCOVERY OF THE SPIRIT-FILLED LIFE?*

Every day can be an exciting adventure for the Christian who knows the reality of being filled with the Holy Spirit and who lives constantly, moment by moment, under His gracious control.

The Bible tells us that there are three kinds of people:

1. NATURAL MAN (one who has not received Christ)

"But a natural man does not accept the things of the Spirit of God; for they are foolishness to him, and he cannot understand them, because they are spiritually appraised" (1 Corinthians 2:14).

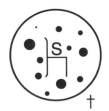

SELF-DIRECTED LIFE
S — Ego or finite self is on the throne
† — Christ is outside the life
● — Interests are controlled by self, often resulting in discord and frustration

2. SPIRITUAL MAN (one who is controlled and empowered by the Holy Spirit)

"But he who is spiritual appraises all things..." (1 Corinthians 2:15).

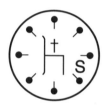

CHRIST-DIRECTED LIFE
† — Christ on the throne of the life
S— Ego or self is dethroned
• — Interests are under control of infinite God, resulting in harmony with God's plan

3. CARNAL MAN (one who has received Christ, but who lives in defeat because he trusts in his own efforts to live the Christian life)

SELF-DIRECTED LIFE
S— Ego or finite self is on the throne
† — Christ is dethroned
• — Interests controlled by self, often resulting in discord and frustration

"And I, brethren, could not speak to you as to spiritual men, but as to carnal men, as to babes in Christ. I gave you milk to drink, not solid food; for you were not yet able to receive it. Indeed, even now you are not yet able, for you are still carnal. For since there is jealousy and strife among you, are you not fleshly, and are you not walking like mere men?" (1 Corinthians 3:1-3).

A. God Has Provided for Us An Abundant and Fruitful Christian Life

Jesus said, "I came that they might have life, and might have it abundantly" (John 10:10).

"I am the vine, you are the branches; he who abides in Me, and I in him, he bears much fruit; for apart from Me you can do nothing" (John 15:5).

"But the fruit of the Spirit is love, joy, peace, patience, kindness, goodness, faithfulness, gentleness, self-control; against such things there is no law" (Galatians 5:22,23).

"But you shall receive power when the Holy Spirit has come upon you; and you shall be My witnesses both in Jerusalem, and in all Judea and Samaria, and even to the remotest part of the earth" (Acts 1:8).

THE SPIRITUAL MAN
Some Personal Traits that Result from Trusting God:

Christ-centered	Love
Empowered by the Holy Spirit	Joy
Introduces others to Christ	Peace
Effective prayer life	Patience
Understands God's Word	Kindness
Trusts God	Goodness
Obeys God	Faithfulness

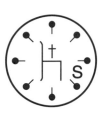

The degree to which these traits are manifested in the life depends upon the extent to which the Christian trusts the Lord with every detail of his life, and upon his maturity in Christ. One who is only beginning to understand the ministry of the Holy Spirit should not be discouraged if he is not as fruitful as more mature Christians who have known and experienced this truth for a longer period.

Why is it that most Christians are not experiencing the abundant life?

B. CARNAL CHRISTIANS CANNOT EXPERIENCE THE ABUNDANT AND FRUITFUL CHRISTIAN LIFE

The carnal man trusts in his own efforts to live the Christian life:

1. He is either uninformed about, or has forgotten, God's love, forgiveness and power (Romans 5:8-10; Hebrews 10:1-25; 1 John 1; 2:1-3; 2 Peter 1:9; Acts 1:8).

2. He has an up-and-down spiritual experience.

3. He cannot understand himself—he wants to do what is right, but cannot.

4. He fails to draw upon the power of the Holy Spirit to live the Christian life.

(1 Corinthians 3:1-3; Romans 7:15-24; 8:7; Galatians 5:16-18)

THE CARNAL MAN

Some or all of the following traits may characterize the Christian who does not fully trust God:

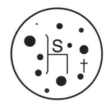

Ignorance of his
   spiritual heritage
Unbelief
Disobedience
Loss of love for God
   and for others
Poor prayer life
No desire for
   Bible study

Legalistic attitude
Discouragement
Impure thoughts
Jealousy
Guilt
Critical spirit
Worry
Frustration
Aimlessness

(The individual who professes to be a Christian but who continues to practice sin should realize that he may not be a Christian at all, according to 1 John 2:3; 3:6,9; Ephesians 5:5.)

The third truth gives us the only solution to this problem...

C. JESUS PROMISED THE ABUNDANT AND FRUITFUL LIFE AS THE RESULT OF BEING FILLED (CONTROLLED AND EMPOWERED) BY THE HOLY SPIRIT

The Spirit-filled life is the Christ-controlled life by which Christ lives His life in and through us in the power of the Holy Spirit (John 15).

1. One becomes a Christian through the ministry of the Holy Spirit, according to John 3:1-8. From the moment of spiritual birth, the Christian is indwelt by the Holy Spirit at all times (John 1:12; Colossians 2:9,10; John 14:16,17). Though all Christians are indwelt by the Holy Spirit, not all Christians are filled (controlled and empowered) by the Holy Spirit.

2. The Holy Spirit is the source of the overflowing life (John 7:37-39).

3. The Holy Spirit came to glorify Christ (John 16:1-5). When one is filled with the Holy Spirit, he is a true disciple of Christ.

4. In His last command before His Ascension, Christ promised the power of the Holy Spirit to enable us to be witnesses for Him (Acts 1:1-9).

How, then, can one be filled with the Holy Spirit?

D. We Are Filled (Controlled And Empowered) by the Holy Spirit By Faith; Then We Can Experience the Abundant and Fruitful Life that Christ Promised To Each Christian

You can appropriate the filling of the Holy Spirit *right now* if you:

1. Sincerely desire to be controlled and empowered by the Holy Spirit (Matthew 5:6; John 7:37-39).

2. Confess your sins.

By faith thank God that He has forgiven all of your sins—past, present, and future—because Christ died for you (Colossians 2:13-15; 1 John 1; 2:1-3; Hebrews 10:1-17).

3. By faith claim the fullness of the Holy Spirit, according to:

a. HIS COMMAND—Be filled with the Spirit. "And do not get drunk with wine, for that is dissipation, but be filled with the Spirit" (Ephesians 5:18).

b. HIS PROMISE—He will always answer when we pray according to His will. "And this is the confidence which we have before Him, that, if we ask anything according to His will, He hears us. And if we know that He hears us in whatever we ask, we know that we have the requests which we have asked from Him" (1 John 5:14,15).

Faith can be expressed through prayer...

How to Pray in Faith to Be Filled with the Holy Spirit
We are filled with the Holy Spirit by faith alone. However, true prayer is one way of expressing your faith. The following is a suggested prayer:

> *Dear Father, I need You. I acknowledge that I have been in control of my life; and that, as a result, I have sinned against You. I thank You that You have forgiven my sins through Christ's death on the cross for me. I now invite Christ to again take control of the throne of my life. Fill me with the Holy Spirit as You commanded me to be filled, and as You promised in your Word that You would do if I asked in faith. I pray this in the name of Jesus. As an expression of my faith, I now thank You for taking control of my life and for filling me with the Holy Spirit.*

Does this prayer express the desire of your heart? If so, bow in prayer and trust God to fill you with the Holy Spirit right now.

How to Know that You are Filled (Controlled And Empowered) by the Holy Spirit
Did you ask God to fill you with the Holy Spirit? Do you know that you are now filled with the Holy Spirit? On what authority?

(On the trustworthiness of God Himself and His Word: Hebrews 11:6; Romans 14:22,23.)

Do not depend upon feelings. The promise of God's Word, not our feelings, is our authority. The Christian lives by faith (trust) in the trustworthiness of God Himself and His Word. This train diagram illustrates the relationship between fact (God and His Word), faith (our trust in God and His Word), and feeling (the result of our faith and obedience) (John 14:21).

The train will run with or without the caboose. However, it would be futile to attempt to pull the train by the caboose. In the same way, we, as Christians, do not depend upon feelings or emotions, but we place our faith (trust) in the trustworthiness of God and the promises of His Word.

How to Walk in the Spirit

Faith (trust in God and His promises) is the only means by which a Christian can live the Spirit-controlled life. As you continue to trust Christ moment by moment:

1. Your life will demonstrate more and more of the fruit of the Spirit (Galatians 5:22,23); and will be more and more conformed to the image of Christ (Romans 12:2; 2 Corinthians 3:18).

2. Your prayer life and study of God's Word will become more meaningful.

3. You will experience His power in witnessing (Acts 1:8).

4. You will be prepared for spiritual conflict against the world (1 John 2:15-17); against the flesh (Galatians 5:16,17); and against Satan (1 Peter 5:7-9; Ephesians 6:10-13).

5. You will experience His power to resist temptation and sin (1 Corinthians 10:13; Philippians 4:13; Ephesians 1:19-23; 6:10; 2 Timothy 1:7; Romans 6;1-16).

Spiritual Breathing

By faith you can continue to experience God's love and forgiveness.

If you become aware of an area of your life (an attitude or an action) that is displeasing to the Lord, even though you are walking with Him and sincerely desiring to serve Him, simply thank God that He has forgiven your sins—past, present and future—on the basis of Christ's death on the cross. Claim His love and forgiveness by faith and continue to have fellowship with Him.

If you retake the throne of your life through sin—a definite act of disobedience—breathe spiritually.

Spiritual Breathing (exhaling the impure and inhaling the pure) is an exercise in faith that enables you to continue to experience God's love and forgiveness.

1. Exhale—confess your sin—agree with God concerning your sin and thank Him for His forgiveness of it, according to 1 John 1:9 and Hebrews 10:1-25. Confession involves repentance—a change in attitude and action.

2. Inhale—surrender the control of your life to Christ, and appropriate (receive) the fullness of the Holy Spirit by faith. Trust that He now controls and empowers you, according to the command of Ephesians 5:18, and the promise of 1 John 5:14,15.

Renew Your Commitment.

Y ou've just finished an inspiring study from **The HomeBuilders Couples Series™**. No doubt you've learned a lot of things about your mate that will help the two of you grow closer together for years to come. You've also learned a lot about God's Word, and how much it means to study the Bible with other couples. But don't let it stop here—lay the next block in the foundation of your marriage by beginning another **HomeBuilders** couples study. It will help you keep your marriage as strong, as dynamic, as solid as the day you said "I do."

Your Mate Is a Gift from God.

Growing together as one begins by accepting your husband or wife as God's perfect provision for your needs —and trusting that He knows what your needs are even better than you do. Receive your mate with open arms, and you'll begin to draw closer together—in incredible, heartfelt new ways.

Building Your Marriage
By Dennis Rainey
Study Guide S411172
Leader's Guide AB026

Turn Conflict into Love and Understanding.

Every marriage has its share of conflict. But you can turn conflict into something positive. Once you get into the habit of being a blessing even when you've been insulted, you'll discover for yourself that the result—a stronger, more exciting marriage—is well worth the effort.

Resolving Conflict in Your Marriage
By Bob & Jan Horner
Study Guide S411202
Leader's Guide AB031

Celebrate and Enjoy Your Differences.

Once you understand that your differences are gifts from God, you'll see how they can help you enjoy each other more and make your relationship fun, healthy and fascinating. You are the unique person who is equipped to complete and fulfill your mate!

Building Teamwork
in Your Marriage
By Robert Lewis
Study Guide S411181
Leader's Guide AB028

Marriage Is God's Workshop for Self-Esteem.

When you both know you are accepted, appreciated and free to risk failure, you'll experience new levels of love and fulfillment—personally and as a couple. It starts by putting past hurts behind you and bringing positive words to your mate that will strengthen, heal and encourage. This study will show you how.

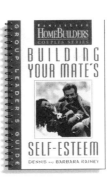

Building Your Mate's
Self-Esteem
By Dennis & Barbara Rainey
Study Guide S411199
Leader's Guide AB030

"A Weekend to Remember"

Every couple has a unique set of needs. The FamilyLife Marriage Conference meets couples' needs by equipping them with proven solutions that address practically every component of "How to Build a Better Marriage." The conference gives you the opportunity to slow down and focus on your spouse and your relationship. You will spend an insightful weekend together, doing fun couples' projects and hearing from dynamic speakers on real-life solutions for building and enhancing oneness in your marriage.

You'll learn:

◆ *Five secrets of successful marriage*
◆ *How to implement oneness in your marriage*
◆ *How to maintain a vital sexual relationship*
◆ *How to handle conflict*
◆ *How to express forgiveness to one another*

Our insightful speaker teams also conduct sessions for:

◆ *Soon-to-be-marrieds*
◆ *Men-only*
◆ *Women-only*

The FamilyLife Marriage Conference
To register or receive a free brochure and schedule, call
FamilyLife at 1-800-333-1433.

A ministry of Campus Crusade for Christ International

Take a Weekend...to Raise Your Children for a Lifetime

Good parents aren't just born that way; they begin with a strong, biblical foundation and then work at improving their parenting skills. That's where we come in.

In one weekend the FamilyLife Parenting Conference will equip you with the principles and tools you need to be more effective parents for a lifetime. Whether you're just getting started or in the turbulent years of adolescence, we'll show you the biblical blueprints for raising your children. You'll hear from dynamic speakers and do fun parenting skills projects designed to help you apply what you've learned. You'll receive proven, effective principles from parents just like you who have dedicated their lives to helping families.

You'll learn how to:

◆ *Build a strong relationship with your child*

◆ *Help your child develop emotional, spiritual and sexual identity*

◆ *Develop moral character in your child*

◆ *Give your child a sense of mission*

◆ *Pass on your values to your child*

The FamilyLife Parenting Conference

To register or receive a free brochure and schedule, call
FamilyLife at 1-800-333-1433.

FAMILYLIFE

A ministry of Campus Crusade for Christ International

FamilyLife Resources

Building Your Mate's Self-Esteem

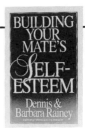

The key to a joy-filled marriage is a strong sense of self-worth in both partners. This practical, best-selling book helps you tap into God's formula for building up your mate. How to overcome problems from the past, how to help your mate conquer self-doubt, how to boost communication, and much more. Creative "Esteem-Builder Projects" will bring immediate results, making your marriage all it can be. The #1 best-seller at FamilyLife Marriage Conferences across America.
Paperback, $8.95

Pulling Weeds, Planting Seeds

Thirty-eight insightful, thought-provoking chapters, laced with humor, show how you can apply the wisdom of God's Word to your life and home. Includes chapters on making your time with your family count, dealing with tough situations at home and at work, living a life of no regrets, and MUCH MORE. These bite-sized, fun-to-read chapters make this great book hard to put down.
Hardcover, $12.95

Staying Close

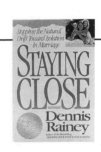

Overcome the isolation that creeps into so many marriages, and watch your marriage blossom! This best-selling book, winner of the 1990 Gold Medallion Award for best book on marriage and family, is packed with practical ideas and HomeBuilders projects to help you experience the oneness God designed for your marriage. How to manage stress. How to handle conflict. How to be a great lover. And much more! Based on 15 years of research and favorite content from the FamilyLife Marriage Conference.
Paperback, $10.95

The Questions Book

Discover the miracle of truly understanding each other. This book will lead you into deeper intimacy and joy by giving you 31 sets of fun, thought-provoking questions you can explore and answer together. Space is provided for you to write your answers. Share your innermost feelings, thoughts, goals, and dreams. This book could lead to the best times you'll ever spend together. **Hardcover, $9.95**

For more information on these and other FamilyLife Resources contact your local Christian retailer or call FamilyLife at 1-800-333-1433.

HomeBuilders Evaluation

Your First Name _____ Last Name _____

Spouse's First Name _____ Wedding Date _____ Your Age _____

Home Phone _____ Work Phone _____

Address _____

City _____ State _____ ZIP Code _____

Full Church Name _____

Church City _____ State _____ May we quote you?

❏ Yes   ❏ No

How would you rate this HomeBuilders Couples study?

	Poor								Excellent	
Overall experience	1	2	3	4	5	6	7	8	9	10
Study Guide	1	2	3	4	5	6	7	8	9	10
Leader's Guide	1	2	3	4	5	6	7	8	9	10

How many HomeBuilders Couples Series have you now participated in ? [   ]

Describe the effect this HomeBuilders study has had on you, your family and your group:

How would you change or improve this HomeBuilders study?

Was this group formed from your: ❏ Church Community ❏ Neighborhood
❏ FamilyLife Marriage Conference ❏ FamilyLife Parenting Conference
❏ Work place   Other: _____

How many people were in this HomeBuilders group? _____

Where did you meet?   ❏ Home (s)   ❏ Church building

How often did your group meet?   ❏ Once/week   ❏ Every other week
❏ Every month   ❏ Other: _____

What day of the week would your group normally meet?

❏ Sunday Morning   ❏ Monday   ❏ Wednesday   ❏ Friday
❏ Sunday Evening   ❏ Tuesday   ❏ Thursday   ❏ Saturday

Have HomeBuilders materials been used in your church? ❏ Yes ❏ No

Have you attended a FamilyLife Conference? ❏ Yes ❏ No

Pastor's First Name _____ Last Name _____

FamilyLife has many other resources for you and your family. Please check if you would like to receive additional information on the following resources:

❏ Other HomeBuilders Couples Series studies   ❏ "FamilyLife Today"
❏ FamilyLife Marriage Conference   radio program
❏ FamilyLife Parenting Conference   ❏ Books, videos and tapes

BUSINESS REPLY MAIL

FIRST-CLASS MAIL   PERMIT NO. 4092   LITTLE ROCK, AR

POSTAGE WILL BE PAID BY ADDRESSEE

FAMILY LIFE
P O BOX 23840
LITTLE ROCK AR 72221-9940